CW01499861

# Limit of Liability/Disclaimer of Warranty

Neither we nor any third parties provide any warranty or guarantee as to the accuracy, timeliness, performance, completeness or suitability of the information and materials found or offered in this study guide for any particular purpose. You acknowledge that such information and materials may contain inaccuracies or errors and we expressly exclude liability for any such inaccuracies or errors to the fullest extent permitted by law.

# How To Use This Book

This study guide will help you pass your state licensing board written exam for nail technology (manicuring) or the National-Interstate Council of State Boards of Cosmetology (NIC) National Nail Technology Theory Exam. To see which states use the NIC National Nail Technology Theory Exam, visit https://nictesting.org/state-agencies-test-administration. Even if your state does not use the NIC exam, this study guide will still help you prepare for your state licensing board exam.

This book contains 2 sections. Section 1 contains questions in exam format. Section 2 contains questions grouped by topics. You may choose to practice by answering the questions in exam format or you may choose to focus on specific topics. Section 1 and Section 2 contain the same questions.

# About the Exam

The following outlines the scope of content covered by the NIC National Nail Technology Theory Examination. The examination is composed of 110 items of which 100 items are weighted and contribute to the candidate's final score.

1A: Scientific Concepts - Infection Control and Safety Practices (15%)
  1. Identify how disease and infection are caused and transmitted
  2. Recognize and utilize infection control principles
      a. Levels of infection control
      b. Process of infection control (e.g., dispensing products, disposal of materials)
  3. Apply blood exposure procedures
  4. Identify adverse reactions to products or services
  5. Utilize Safety Data Sheets (SDS)
  6. Identify ways to prevent work injuries (e.g., ventilation, ergonomics)

1B: Scientific Concepts - Anatomy and Physiology (15%)
  1. Identify functions, parts, and structure of the:
      a. nails
      b. skin
  2. Recognize disorders and diseases of the:
      a. nails
      b. skin
  3. Recognize signs and symptoms of disorders, diseases, and conditions of the:
      a. nails
      b. skin
  4. Identify bones of the:
      a. arms and hands
      b. legs and feet
  5. Identify muscles and recognize their functions in the:
      a. arms and hands
      b. legs and feet

1C: Scientific Concepts - Chemistry of Nail Products (10%)
  1. Explain purpose and effects of product ingredients
  2. Recognize interaction between chemicals
  3. Recognize physical changes
  4. Recognize chemical reactions

2A: Nail Technology Procedures - Client Consultation and Documentation (5%)
  1. Identify elements of a client consultation and documentation
  2. Evaluate condition of client's nails and skin
  3. Recognize conditions that would prohibit service (contraindications)
  4. Determine services or products

2B: Nail Technology Procedures - Nail Service Tools (8%)
1. Identify purpose and function of:
a. Nail equipment (e.g., electric file, pedicure basin)
b. Nail implements (e.g., nail clippers, cuticle pusher)
c. Nail supplies and materials (e.g., cotton, buffer)
d. Nail products (e.g., polish, lotion)
2. Follow practices for safe use of tools

2C: Nail Technology Procedures - Nail Service Preparation (5%)
1. Perform set-up of workstation service area
2. Perform client and practitioner sanitation

2D: Nail Technology Procedures - Manicure and Pedicure Services (18%)
1. Perform procedures for basic manicure and/or pedicure service
a. Trim and shape nails
b. Soak
c. Cuticle maintenance
d. Cleanse nails
e. Buff nails
f. Exfoliate
g. Perform basic massage
1. Identify mechanics of massage movements
a. Effleurage
b. Petrissage
c. Friction
d. Tapotement
2. Recognize effects of massage types
a. Effleurage
b. Petrissage
c. Friction
d. Tapotement
h. Completion of service
2. Recognize purpose and procedures for add-on services
a. Paraffin
b. Masks and essential oils
c. Gel polish
d. Thermal (e.g., stone, towel)

2E: Nail Technology Procedures - Perform Application Maintenance and Removal Procedures for Nail Enhancement Services (20%)
1. Nail tip
2. Acrylics
3. Light-cured gels

4. Powder dip

2F: Nail Technology Procedures - Perform Post-Service Procedures (4%)

# Section 1

# Practice Exam 1

1. Soaking foot spas and basins in disinfectant overnight should be done
   a. At least once a week
   b. At least twice a week
   c. At least once every 2 weeks
   d. At least once a month
2. Which nail condition is associated with brittle nails with lengthwise ridges?
   a. Beau's line
   b. Plicatured nail
   c. Eggshell nails
   d. Melanonychia
   e. Onychorrhexis
3. What is responsible for skin pigment?
   a. Elastin
   b. Keratin
   c. Collagen
   d. Melanocytes
4. Sodium hydroxide or lye is an
   a. Acid
   b. Alkali
5. Standard precautions involve which of the following? Select all that apply.
   a. Washing hands
   b. Wearing gloves when there is a potential for blood exposure
   c. Proper disposal of sharp instruments
   d. Proper disposal of items contaminated with blood and/or body fluids
   e. Wearing masks when there is a potential for exposure to airborne pathogens
6. Nail polish is an example of:
   a. An emulsion
   b. A surfactant
   c. A suspension
   d. All of the above
7. Which of the following is highly resistant to antibiotics?
   a. Streptococci
   b. Bacilli
   c. Spirilla
   d. MRSA
8. Which of the following is composed of specialized tissues that perform specific functions?
   a. Cells
   b. Nails
   c. Hair
   d. Stomach

9. In a massage technique called _____, skin tissue is lifted and pressed together.
   a. Effleurage
   b. Petrissage
   c. Tapotement
   d. Vibration

10. Another word for curing is _____.
   a. Evaporation
   b. Preservation
   c. Scarification
   d. Polymerization

11. How should implements be immersed in disinfection containers? Select all that apply.
   a. Immerse only parts of the implements that come into contact with clients
   b. Immerse all implements completely, except for the handles so that you can remove the implements without coming into contact with the disinfectant
   c. Immerse all implements completely
   d. All disinfectant containers must have lids to prevent the disinfectant solution from being contaminated.

12. When dealing with a dissatisfied client, you should
   a. Try to make the client happy, at all cost
   b. Inform the client on why you are right
   c. Try to make the client happy, within reason
   d. Immediately ask them to speak to the salon manager

13. Nails should be soaked in water before filing.
   a. True
   b. False

14. What is used as a guide to extend the nail enhancement beyond the fingertip?
   a. Nail form
   b. A ruler
   c. Metal pusher
   d. Wooden pusher

15. What is the first step in performing a manicure?
   a. Shape the nails
   b. Soften the cuticles
   c. Clean under free edge
   d. Remove old polish

16. After service, a dappen dish should be cleaned with
   a. Alcohol
   b. Acetone
   c. Hot water
   d. A lint free towel

17. When making retail recommendations, what should you explain to the client? Select all that apply.
   a. What is being recommended
   b. Why you are recommending a product

c. How the product should be used at home

d. Who else uses the product

18. Nail enhancements should be serviced

    a. After 1 or more weeks

    b. After 2 or more weeks

    c. After 3 or more weeks

    d. After 4 or more weeks

19. Nail tips that are _____ require less filing on natural nails after application.

    a. Pre-beveled

    b. Pre-cut

    c. Well-less

    d. All of the above

20. What are the group of five bones of the hand between the wrist and the fingers?

    a. Carpus

    b. Metacarpus

    c. Phalanges

    d. None of the above

21. UV gloss gels can be used over monomer and polymer enhancements.

    a. True

    b. False

22. A communal nail brush can be used by multiple clients to wash their hands.

    a. True

    b. False

23. To prevent damaging nail wraps when removing old polish, use

    a. A file to remove the old polish

    b. Use a non-acetone polish remover

    c. Use an acetone polish remover

    d. Use a resin softener first

24. Cutting tips with fingernail or toenail clippers can weaken tips and cause tips to crack.

    a. True

    b. False

25. High vibration during use of an electric file can ? Select all that apply.

    a. Cause microshattering of nail enhancement products

    b. Be harmful to the technicians hand, wrist, and arm

    c. Lead to the development of carpal tunnel syndrome

    d. None of the above

26. To repair tip separation, you must first remove the old nail enhancement product.

    a. True

    b. False

27. What are some "rings of fire" causes? Select all that apply.

    a. Keeping the bit parallel to the nail

    b. Using a flat tipped bit at an angle

    c. Using too low of a speed

    d. Not applying enough pressure

28. What are some ways to prevent grabbing during filing? Select all that apply.
    a. Keep the bit parallel to the nail
    b. Keep the bit angled to the nail
    c. Angle the bit to file the sides of the nail
    d. Angle the finger to file the sides of the nail
    e. Use bits with rounded ends
29. What are some causes of heat during filing? Select all that apply.
    a. Too much pressure
    b. Incorrect speed (RPM)
    c. Leaving the bit in one place for too long
    d. Using sanders or sleeves
    e. Lifting the bit too frequently
30. What resin should be used for clients who want colored polish or gel polish over an enhancement?
    a. Clear resin
    b. Pink resin
    c. White pigmented resin
    d. Tan resin
31. You should use nippers to trim or remove loose nail enhancement products.
    a. True
    b. False
32. _____ increase the rate at which chemical reactions occur.
    a. Thermal initiators
    b. Photoinitiators
    c. Catalysts
    d. Oligomers
33. Nerves and blood vessels are found in the nail
    a. Bed
    b. Wall
    c. Plate
    d. Grooves
34. During nail enhancement maintenance, what type of bit should be used to prepare for a backfill?
    a. Medium grit bit with a round-tipped edge
    b. Medium grit bit with a flat tipped edge
    c. Fine grit bit with a round-tipped edge
    d. Fine grit bit with a flat tipped edge
35. When applying UV gel, patting the brush or pressing too hard can? Select all that apply.
    a. Cause the UV gel to dry too quickly
    b. Introduce air into the gel
    c. Weaken the gel enhancement
    d. Make the gel enhancement too hard
36. High shine bits or buffer bits are single use only.
    a. True

b. False

37. Nail tips have a shallow depression called a _____.
    a. Position stop
    b. Tip point
    c. Well
    d. Demarcation line

38. Which electric file bits should never be used on natural nails?
    a. Diamond bits
    b. Carbide bits
    c. Barrel bits
    d. UNC bits

39. The strongest nail wrap material is
    a. Silk
    b. Linen
    c. Fiberglass
    d. Paper

40. What should be used to correct flat fingernails?
    a. UV bonding gels
    b. UV building gels
    c. UV self leveling gels
    d. UV gel polish

41. To speed up the hardening process of a wrap resin or adhesive overlay, you should use
    a. A nail dehydrator
    b. UV lights
    c. A wrap resin accelerator or activator
    d. All of the above

42. In addition to the standard implements on a manicuring table, what supplies are needed for a nail tip application procedure? Select all that apply.
    a. Nail tips
    b. Nail tip adhesive
    c. Acetone
    d. Abrasive boards
    e. Tip cutter
    f. Wrap resin
    g. Buffer block
    h. Nail dehydrator

43. After each use, manicuring implements should be
    a. wiped with a towel
    b. wiped with a tissue
    c. cleansed and disinfected
    d. placed in dry storage

44. Ingrown nails are also known as
    a. Onychia
    b. Onychocryptosis

    c. Onychomadesis

    d. Onychomycosis.

45. Where should all manicuring cosmetic supplies be kept when not being used?

    a. On a clean shelf

    b. On the manicuring table

    c. In a clean manicuring kit

    d. In clean, closed containers

46. What is the actively growing part of the nail?

    a. Lunula

    b. Matrix

    c. Mantle

    d. Free edge

47. Which abrasive is used to shorten and shape natural nails?

    a. A lower grit abrasive

    b. A medium grit abrasive

    c. A higher grit abrasive

    d. A fine grit abrasive

48. When performing pedicures, you should work from

    a. Little toe to big toe

    b. Big toe to little toe

49. Before a paraffin wax treatment, a heat tolerance test should be performed by

    a. Sticking your hands into the paraffin wax

    b. Sticking your client's hands into the paraffin wax

    c. Pouring a little wax out to see if it will solidify within 30 seconds

    d. Drop a 1 inch size circle on the client's hands to see if it is well tolerated

50. Which muscles help bend the foot down? Select all that apply.

    a. Extensor digitorum longus

    b. Tibialis anterior

    c. Peroneus brevis

    d. Soleus

51. A 2 inch thick bed of activated carbon filter can properly absorb vapors and remove them from the salon air.

    a. True

    b. False

52. What massage technique is most often used by nail technicians?

    a. Effleurage

    b. Petrissage

    c. Tapotement

    d. Vibration

53. If a client decides to get a paraffin wax treatment before a manicure, soaking the hands in water is not necessary because the paraffin treatment already softens the skin.

    a. True

    b. False

54. Some conditions require multiple appointments to resolve the issue. This is called a
   a. Set pedicure
   b. Multiple service pedicure
   c. Complex pedicure
   d. Series pedicure
55. Applying nail polish close to the eponychium will cause the polish to lift within a few days.
   a. True
   b. False
56. Before a pedicure appointment, women should avoid shaving their legs within ____ hours before the appointment.
   a. 12
   b. 24
   c. 48
   d. There is no need to avoid shaving
57. Sea sand, ground apricot kernels, and jojoba beads are examples of
   a. Acids
   b. Bases
   c. Exfoliating agents
   d. Moisturizers
58. Toe separators are single use items.
   a. True
   b. False
59. Which nail shape may break more easily and is more difficult to maintain?
   a. Square
   b. Squoval
   c. Round
   d. Oval
   e. Pointed
60. Which of the following muscle types are under voluntary control? Select all that apply.
   a. Smooth
   b. Striated
   c. Non-striated
   d. Cardiac
61. Benefits of a paraffin bath include ? Select all that apply.
   a. Increased moisturization
   b. Reduced pain and inflammation
   c. Increased circulation to joins
   d. Warmth and relaxation
62. When clipping long nails,
   a. Clip from one side to the other side
   b. Clip the sides and center in one clip
   c. Clip from the sides, clipping towards the center
63. Which of the following has the correct order of steps for performing a manicure?

a. Remove polish from nails; apply cuticle remover, remove cuticles, and wash cuticle remover from hands; file and shape nails; soak the fingers; brush the nails with a nail brush; dry the hands; buff the nails; apply nail oil to nails; lotion and massage the hands; remove oil or lotion from the nail plate; apply polish

b. Remove polish from nails; file and shape nails; soak the fingers; brush the nails with a nail brush; dry the hands; apply cuticle remover, remove cuticles, and wash cuticle remover from hands; buff the nails; apply nail oil to nails; lotion and massage the hands; remove oil or lotion from the nail plate; apply polish

c. Remove polish from nails; file and shape nails; soak the fingers; apply nail oil to nails; brush the nails with a nail brush; dry the hands; apply cuticle remover, remove cuticles, and wash cuticle remover from hands; buff the nails; lotion and massage the hands; remove oil or lotion from the nail plate; apply polish

d. Remove polish from nails; file and shape nails; soak the fingers; dry the hands; brush the nails with a nail brush; apply cuticle remover, remove cuticles, and wash cuticle remover from hands; buff the nails; apply nail oil to nails; lotion and massage the hands; remove oil or lotion from the nail plate; apply polish

64. The manicure table should be cleaned and disinfected as part of the pre-service procedure.
   a. True
   b. False

65. Hands should be washed for a minimum of
   a. 15 seconds
   b. 20 seconds
   c. 30 seconds
   d. 60 seconds

66. Pumice stone is used in pedicuring as
   a. an abrasive
   b. a bleach
   c. a lubricant
   d. an astringent

67. What product should be applied to brittle nails to help strengthen the nail?
   a. Protein hardeners
   b. Methylene glycol hardeners
   c. Dimethylurea hardeners
   d. B and C

68. Complete replacement of a fingernail takes about
   a. 1 to 2 months
   b. 3 months
   c. 4 to 6 months
   d. 12 months

69. What should be applied to nails to prevent natural nail discoloration or yellowish discoloration of nail polish?
   a. Nail oils
   b. Nail hardener

     c. Base coat

     d. Top coat

70. Excessive use of cuticle removers can lead to

     a. Dry skin

     b. Dry eponychium

     c. Hangnails

     d. A and B

     e. A,B, and C

71. Which product is designed to be absorbed into nails to make them more flexible?

     a. Nail creams

     b. Nail oils

     c. Nail polish remover

     d. Nail soap

72. Which of the following are true statements? Select all that apply.

     a. Gloves must be worn when servicing a client.

     b. A new set of gloves must be used for each client.

     c. If performing both a manicure and pedicure for a single client, a new set of gloves must be worn for each service.

     d. Hands should be washed or antimicrobial gel should be applied after removing gloves and before putting on new gloves.

73. When cleaning and disinfecting pipeless foot spas, the impeller, footplate, and any other removable components must be removed, cleaned, and disinfected after every client.

     a. True

     b. False

74. Acetone based polish removers dissolve polish quicker than non-acetone based polish removers.

     a. True

     b. False

75. When using two-way or three-way buffers, start with the lowest grit surface.

     a. True

     b. False

76. Which of the following should you do during the client consultation? Select all that apply.

     a. Review the client intake form.

     b. Assess your client's hands and nails

     c. Ask about your client's career

     d. Ask about your client's hobbies

     e. Upsell services

77. Hands should be washed a minimum of

     a. 10 seconds

     b. 15 seconds

     c. 20 seconds

     d. 30 seconds

78. When meeting an older client for the first time, you should

     a. Address them by their first name

b. Address them by the honorific (e.g. "Mrs"/"Mr")

c. Address them as "Sir" or "M'am"

d. Asked them how they'd like to be addressed

79. Liquid soaps can neutralize callus softeners.

a. True

b. False

80. N95 masks are effective against vapors.

a. True

b. False

81. Colored polymer powders are an example of

a. A pure substance

b. A physical mixture

c. A suspension

d. None of the above

82. Which of the following is used in nail polish dryers and skin protectants?

a. Silicone

b. Glycerin

c. VOCs

d. All of the above

83. Which of the following uses thermal initiators?

a. UV curing products

b. Monomer liquid systems

c. Polymer powder systems

d. B and C

e. All of the above

84. Volatile organic compounds (VOCs) can be found in ? Select all that apply

a. Nail polish

b. Polish removers

c. Base and top coats

d. None of the above

85. Water is a _____.

a. Solution

b. Solute

c. Solvent

d. All of the above.

86. A _____ change is a change in the form of a substance.

a. Physical

b. Chemical

87. Which muscles are used to form a straight line with the wrist, hand, and fingers?

a. Extensors

b. Flexors

c. Pronators

d. Supinator

88. Common places for skin allergies to occur include which of the following? Select all that apply.
   a. Between a nail technician's thumb and pointer finger
   b. On a nail technician's wrist, palm, or back of the hand
   c. On a nail technician's face
   d. On a client's eponychium, fingertips, or nail bed
89. Which one of the following is a condition in which the cuticle splits around the nail?
   a. Hangnails
   b. Pterygium
   c. Onychophagy
   d. Onychorrhexis
90. Contact dermatitis is an avoidable skin disease.
   a. True
   b. False
91. Which of the following can lead to improper curing of UV gels? Select all that apply.
   a. Applying products too thickly
   b. Not enough time under the UV lamp
   c. Dirty UV lamps
   d. Using a UV lamp not specifically designated for the UV gel system
92. The nail plate is non porous.
   a. True
   b. False
93. The white, half-mooned shape at the bottom of the nail plate is called
   a. The free edge
   b. The closed edge
   c. The open edge
   d. The lunula
94. The skin is an example of what type of tissue?
   a. Adipose
   b. Connective
   c. Epithelial
   d. Muscle
   e. Nerve
95. Nail technicians are allowed to push back, as well as, cut the eponychium.
   a. True
   b. False
96. How should you deal with tardy clients? Select all that apply.
   a. Follow the salons appointment policies
   b. If you client is late, but you can fit them in without jeopardizing other appointments, let the client know even though they are late, you will still able to service them
   c. If the client is frequently late for their appointments, schedule their appointment for the end of the day or tell them to arrive earlier than their actual appointment time

97. Which of the following are reusable items? Select all that apply.
   a. Towels
   b. Bits
   c. Pumice stone
   d. Some buffers
   e. Wooden sticks

98. As part of the SDS categories, Disposal Consideration includes proper disposal and
   a. Chemical hazards
   b. Disposal restrictions
   c. Restrictions on transportation
   d. All of the above

99. An antiseptic is used in manicuring to
   a. bleach the nails
   b. treat minor cuts
   c. smooth corrugated nails
   d. give the nails a high sheen

100. A _____ is used to keep a record of equipment usage, cleaning, and disinfecting.
   a. Notebook
   b. Spreadsheet
   c. Filing system
   d. Logbook

101. Which type of hepatitis are you most likely to encounter at a salon?
   a. Hepatitis A
   b. Hepatitis B
   c. Hepatitis C
   d. B & C

102. Hinged instruments should be in the _____ position before being immersed in disinfectant solution.
   a. Open
   b. Closed

103. A(n) _____ is when an employee comes into contact with potentially infectious material.
   a. Accident
   b. Emergency
   c. Exposure incident
   d. Hazmat exposure

104. The most popular nail shape for men is
   a. Square
   b. Round
   c. Oval
   d. Pointed

105. Hand sanitizers or antiseptics can be used in place of hand washing.
   a. True
   b. False

106. If a client brings in their own tools and implements, you must disinfect their tools and implements before using them on the client.
   a. True
   b. False
107. You should talk to your clients during massages to help them relax.
   a. True
   b. False
108. Porous items that have been exposed to broken skin, blood, or body fluids must be thrown away.
   a. True
   b. False
109. During post-service procedures, information should be recorded in a
   a. Client record form
   b. Client intake form
   c. Client questionnaire
   d. Client survey
110. Which bacteria is most likely to cause diseases such as pneumonia?
   a. Staphylococci
   b. Streptococci
   c. Diplococci
   d. Bacilli
   e. Spirilla

# Practice Exam 2

1. Which of the following should NOT be used to disinfect pedicure tubs?
   a. Quats
   b. Phenolics
   c. Bleach
   d. None of the above

2. Damage to the hyponychium can cause which of the following?
   a. Separation between the nail plate and nail bed
   b. Increase risk of infection underneath the nail plate
   c. A and B
   d. None of the above

3. Which of the following is used as a solvent as well as a moisturizer?
   a. Silicone
   b. Glycerin
   c. VOCs
   d. All of the above

4. Extra precaution should be taken when working with clients that have which of the following conditions? Select all that apply.
   a. Arthritis
   b. Circulatory diseases
   c. Diabetes
   d. High blood pressure

5. Hives are examples of what type of primary skin lesions?
   a. Cyst
   b. Macule
   c. Vesicle
   d. Wheal

6. Bacteria on a nail polish brush can be transferred to another client's nails if the nail polish brush is immediately used.
   a. True
   b. False

7. Free edge separation from nail enhancement products can be caused by ? Select all that apply.
   a. Nail enhancement product breakdown
   b. Aging of the nail enhancement product
   c. A client being hard on the nails
   d. Only A and B

8. During a paraffin wax treatment, the paraffin should remain on the hands for
   a. 5 to 10 minutes
   b. 15 to 20 minutes
   c. 25 to 30 minutes
   d. 60 minutes

9. When not in use, UV brushes and gel containers should be ? Select all that apply.

a. Stored away from windows
b. Stored away from all sources of UV light
c. Exposed to sunlight to prevent bacterial growth
d. Stored away from full spectrum lights

10. Which type of hepatitis are you most likely to encounter at a salon?
    a. Hepatitis A
    b. Hepatitis B
    c. Hepatitis C
    d. B & C

11. Complete replacement of a fingernail takes about
    a. 1 to 2 months
    b. 3 months
    c. 4 to 6 months
    d. 12 months

12. Common places for skin allergies to occur include which of the following? Select all that apply.
    a. Between a nail technician's thumb and pointer finger
    b. On a nail technician's wrist, palm, or back of the hand
    c. On a nail technician's face
    d. On a client's eponychium, fingertips, or nail bed

13. Which of the following is used in nail polish dryers and skin protectants?
    a. Silicone
    b. Glycerin
    c. VOCs
    d. All of the above

14. Which of the following are true statements? Select all that apply.
    a. Gloves must be worn when servicing a client.
    b. A new set of gloves must be used for each client.
    c. If performing both a manicure and pedicure for a single client, a new set of gloves must be worn for each service.
    d. Hands should be washed or antimicrobial gel should be applied after removing gloves and before putting on new gloves.

15. The manicure table should be cleaned and disinfected as part of the pre-service procedure.
    a. True
    b. False

16. Select all statements that are true.
    a. Warts are highly contagious parasites.
    b. Warts are highly contagious viruses.
    c. Warts are most commonly found on the bottom of the feet or on the fingers or palms.
    d. None of the above.

17. In a massage technique called _____, skin tissue is lifted and pressed together.
    a. Effleurage

    b. Petrissage

    c. Tapotement

    d. Vibration

18. Which electric file bits should never be used on natural nails?

    a. Diamond bits

    b. Carbide bits

    c. Barrel bits

    d. UNC bits

19. What are some "rings of fire" causes? Select all that apply.

    a. Keeping the bit parallel to the nail

    b. Using a flat tipped bit at an angle

    c. Using too low of a speed

    d. Not applying enough pressure

20. With proper home maintenance, how long should a nail polish application last?

    a. 3 to 5 days

    b. 7 to 10 days

    c. 14 to 21 days

    d. 21 to 31 days

21. You must wash your hands after removing gloves.

    a. True

    b. False

22. Clients should pay

    a. Before a procedure is performed

    b. After a procedure is performed

23. Unless otherwise specified by the manufacturer, a disinfectant contact time of ____ minutes is required for all items.

    a. 5

    b. 10

    c. 15

    d. 20

24. Nail plate cells are formed in the

    a. Nail bed

    b. Nail fold

    c. Matrix

    d. Free edge.

25. The first step in the nail tip removal procedure is to cut off the nail tip.

    a. True

    b. False

26. The advantages of nail wraps are they _____. Select all that apply.

    a. Decrease the time between maintenance periods

    b. Can increase the strength and durability of nail tips.

    c. Can be used to repair or strengthen natural nails

    d. Can be used to create nail extensions

27. Which UV gel is used to repair a crack in a nail enhancement?

a. UV bonding gels

b. UV building gels

c. UV self leveling gels

d. UV gel polishes

28. During nail wrap application, wrap resin should be applied _____.

    a. Over the entire surface of the nail and tip

    b. Over the entire surface of the nail

    c. Over the entire surface of the tip

    d. Where the nail tip meets the natural nail

29. What are the ways monomer liquid and polymer powder can be applied? Select all that apply.

    a. They can be applied as a protective overlay on the natural nail

    b. They can be applied over a nail tip

    c. They can be used to create a nail extension

    d. They can be used to hydrate the nail

30. What layer of the skin is fat tissue found in?

    a. Epidermis

    b. Dermis

    c. Subcutaneous

31. In a massage technique called _____, the skin is rapidly tapped or striked by the hand.

    a. Effleurage

    b. Petrissage

    c. Tapotement

    d. Vibration

32. Which bit works best for smoothing calluses?

    a. Small and large barrel bits

    b. Maintenance bits

    c. Needle bits

    d. Pedicure bits

33. Applying nail enhancement products over wet nail primers can cause the nail enhancement product to discolor and break down.

    a. True

    b. False

34. Which UV gel is used to increase adhesion to the natural nail?

    a. UV bonding gels

    b. UV building gels

    c. UV self leveling gels

    d. UV gel polishes

35. A(n) _____ is a pooling of blood underneath the skin or nails.

    a. Keloid

    b. Hematoma

    c. Ulcer

    d. Fissure

    e. Excoriation

f. Scale

36. What consistency should the product bead have?
    a. Dry
    b. Wet
    c. Medium to dry
    d. Medium to wet

37. The amount of colored pigment in a gel is called
    a. Viscosity
    b. Pigmentation
    c. Clarity
    d. Opacity

38. UV gel polishes may be used on natural nails.
    a. True
    b. False

39. Monomer liquid and polymer power should be stored ____. Select all that apply.
    a. Away from each other
    b. In a covered container
    c. In a cool, dark area
    d. Near heat

40. What are some reasons why you should avoid using large brushes when working with monomer liquid and polymer powder? Select all that apply.
    a. Large brushes increase the risk that the brush touches the skin
    b. Large brushes can hold too much liquid
    c. Large brushes can increase the risk of improper liquid and powder ratio
    d. Only A and B

41. As nail enhancement products age, they can become brittle and develop tiny cracks. This is known as
    a. Brittle nails
    b. Cracked nails
    c. Macroshattering
    d. Microshattering

42. Monomer liquid should be poured into
    a. Open mouthed jars
    b. Containers with large openings
    c. A shallow bowl
    d. A dappen dish

43. What resin should be used for clients who want French or American manicure finish without using nail lacquer?
    a. Clear resin
    b. Pink resin
    c. White pigmented resin
    d. Pink resin and white pigmented resin

44. Nail wraps are a type of
    a. Nail tip

    b. Overlay

    c. Nail resin

    d. Nail adhesive

45. The SDS Regulatory Information category lists OSHA's permissible exposure limits.

    a. True

    b. False

46. Nail tips are strong enough to wear on their own.

    a. True

    b. False

47. Which muscle is used to move the big toe?

    a. Flexor digiti minimi

    b. Flexor digitorum brevis

    c. Abductor hallucis

    d. Abductor digiti minimi

48. When applying UV or LED gel to the natural nail,

    a. Only the first layer of product needs to be cured

    b. Only the last layer of product needs to be cured

    c. Only the first and last layers of product needs to be cured

    d. Each layer of product needs to be cured

49. To remove nail oil from the nail plates, _____. Select all that apply.

    a. Use cotton saturated with alcohol

    b. Use cotton saturated with acetone or polish remover

    c. Use cotton saturated with water

    d. Use cotton saturated with cuticle remover

50. Before massaging the hands, you should apply enough lotion

    a. To moisturize the hands

    b. To make the hands very slippery

    c. To prevent skin drag

51. To help remove or lessen yellow stains or discoloration of the nails,

    a. Apply a clear coat to the nails

    b. Apply nail bleach

    c. Apply nail oil

    d. None of the above

52. When brushing nails with a nail brush, you should

    a. Use downward strokes, starting from the first knuckle and brushing towards the fingertips.

    b. Use upward strokes, starting from the fingertips and brushing towards the first knuckle

    c. Brush horizontally across the nail plate

    d. A and B

53. When using curettes, the bowl of the curette should face _____ the skin.

    a. Away from

    b. Toward

54. The _____ contains no blood vessels.

a. Dermis

b. Epidermis

55. According to client surveys, the most enjoyable part of a pedicure is

a. Having clean nails

b. Having pretty nails

c. The massage

d. Having calluses removed

56. Before applying nail polish, you should ask clients to put on any jewelry or outerwear they took off before service.

a. True

b. False

57. Paraffin wax should be maintained at a temperature

a. Below 100F

b. Between 125 and 132F

c. Between 132 and 140F

d. Above 140F

58. When filing nails, you should

a. Use a sawing back and forth motion

b. File into the corners of the nails

c. File from one side to the center and then file from the other side to the center

d. B and C

59. When performing a manicure, you should work from

a. Pinky finger to thumb finger

b. Thumb finger to pinky finger

60. What should be used to remove debris for toe nail folds, eponychium, and hyponychium areas?

a. Toenail clippers

b. Toenail nippers

c. Curettes

d. Nail rasp

61. Skin and nails are a part of which body system?

a. Lymphatic

b. Endocrine

c. Integumentary

d. Excretory

62. Hot stones can transfer MRSA infections between clients.

a. True

b. False

63. Which tool can be used to reduce and smooth foot calluses?

a. Curettes

b. Nail rasp

c. Toenail nippers

d. Pedicure paddles

64. A complete manicured nail typically has how many coats?

a. 1
b. 2
c. 3
d. 4

65. Which tool can be used to reduce the sides of the free edge to reduce chances of an ingrown nail?
    a. Toenail clippers
    b. Nail rasp
    c. Foot files or pedicure paddles
    d. Nail files

66. Lamps attached to the manicuring table should use a fluorescent bulb or a _____ incandescent bulb.
    a. 20 to 40 watt
    b. 40 to 60 watt
    c. 60 to 80 watt
    d. 80 to 100 watt

67. The correct order of steps for cleaning and disinfecting implements are
    a. Put on gloves, soak implements in disinfectant, wash implements with soap, rinse implements with warm water and dry implements, store implements in a clean and dry container, remove gloves and wash your hands
    b. Put on gloves, wash implements with soap, rinse implements with warm water, soak implements in disinfectant, rinse and dry implements, remove gloves and wash your hands, store implements in a clean and dry container
    c. Wash implements with soap, rinse implements with warm water, put on gloves, soak implements in disinfectant, rinse and dry implements, store implements in a clean and dry container, remove gloves and wash your hands
    d. Put on gloves, wash implements with soap, rinse implements with warm water, soak implements in disinfectant, rinse and dry implements, store implements in a clean and dry container, remove gloves and wash your hands

68. Disinfected implements should be
    a. Left on an open shelf and allowed to air dry
    b. Stored in a clean and dry container until needed
    c. Wrapped in a towel and stored on an open shelf

69. After washing and drying your hands, you should use a towel (paper or cloth) to open the door.
    a. True
    b. False

70. Fine grit abrasives have
    a. Grits of 180 or lower
    b. Grits of 180
    c. Grits between 180 and 240
    d. Grits of 240 or higher

71. Which type of hepatitis virus is most difficult to kill on a surface?
    a. Hepatitis A

b. Hepatitis B

c. Hepatitis C

d. A & B

72. The process of preparing a nail file for use by using another clean file to rub away sharp edges is called

    a. Abrasive conditioning

    b. File prepping

    c. File polishing

    d. None of the above

73. Albinism is associated with _____.

    a. Chloasma

    b. Lentigines

    c. Leukoderma

    d. Nevus

74. What product should be used to prevent nail polish from chipping?

    a. Nail oils

    b. Nail hardener

    c. Base coat

    d. Top coat

75. Which of the following statements is true?

    a. The lower the grit, the larger the abrasive particles; make the file less abrasive.

    b. The lower the grit, the larger the abrasive particles; making the file more abrasive.

    c. The lower the grit, the smaller the abrasive particles; making the file less abrasive.

    d. The lower the grit, the smaller the abrasive particles; making the file more abrasive.

76. Nail files and buffers are considered multi-use items.

    a. True

    b. False

77. Nail polish should be shaken often to ensure an even polish consistency.

    a. True

    b. False

78. What are the functions of the skin? Select all that apply.

    a. Protection

    b. Sensation

    c. Heat regulation

    d. Excretion

    e. Secretion

79. Which of the following do not harbor or support microbial growth? Select all that apply.

    a. Nail polish

    b. Monomers

    c. Polymers

    d. UV gels

e. Nail primers

f. Nail oil

80. When working with nail nippers, the _____ should be placed on the box joint to help control the blade.

    a. Thumb

    b. Index finger

    c. Middle finger

    d. Index and middle finger

81. When dealing with a scheduling mix-up, you should

    a. Try to determine who is at fault to see who is responsible for fixing the mix-up

    b. Do not worry about who is at fault and work on resolving the situation

    c. Ignore the mix-up and try to squeeze the client into the schedule

82. Foot and leg massages are contraindicated in patients with which of the following? Select all that apply.

    a. Diabetes

    b. Hypertension

    c. Varicose veins

    d. Hay fever

83. You should recommend nail penetrating oils to clients to keep natural and enhanced nails moisturized and flexible.

    a. True

    b. False

84. Acetone is inflammable.

    a. True

    b. False

85. When nail problems occur, they are most likely due to ?

    a. Improper nail plate preparation

    b. Improper application or maintenance of nail products

    c. Improper removal of nail products

    d. All of the above

86. Thermal initiators get energy when exposed to UV.

    a. True

    b. False

87. Products made from _____ are harder to dissolve.

    a. Non cross-linked polymers

    b. Cross-linked polymers

88. Nail polishes contain _____ which prevent fading and discoloration from sunlight.

    a. Acrylics

    b. Adhesives

    c. UV stabilizers

    d. Plasticizers

89. Select all the reasons why Methyl methacrylate monomer (MMA) should not be used in nail salons.

    a. MMA is toxic.

b. MMA nail products do not adhere well to the nail plate unless the nail plate has been shredded.

c. MMA creates nails that are hard and difficult to break.

d. MMA is very difficult to remove.

e. The FDA says not to use it.

90. Water and oil are examples of _____ liquids.

a. Miscible

b. Immiscible

91. All nail enhancements and nail adhesives are made from acrylics.

a. True

b. False

92. What is responsible for UV gels thick and sticky consistency and ability to harden quickly?

a. Oligomers

b. Polymers

c. Methyl methacrylate monomer

d. None of the above

93. Damage to the _____ can change the shape and thickness of the nail plate.

a. Hyponychium

b. Eponychium

c. Matrix

94. The live tissue attached to the nail plate is called the:

a. Cuticle

b. Eponychium

95. A 36 watt UV lamp unit will emit 36 watts of UV energy.

a. True

b. False

96. Contact dermatitis can be caused by which of the following? Select all that apply.

a. Prolonged and repeated contact with substances

b. Improper product consistency

c. Undercuring UV or LED gel enhancements

d. Exposure to allergy causing substances

97. Acne is usually the result of a blocked _____.

a. Sudoriferous gland

b. Sebaceous gland

c. Nerve

d. None of the above

98. The foot is composed of which of the following? Select all that apply.

a. Carpus

b. Tarsals

c. Metacarpus

d. Metatarsals

e. Phalanges

99. Multi-use items that have been exposed to blood or body fluids must be thrown away.
   a. True
   b. False
100. Which of the following statements is NOT true? Select all that apply.
   a. Always wear gloves and safety glasses when mixing disinfectants.
   b. Always use tongs or gloves to remove items from disinfectants
   c. Always add a disinfectant to water to prevent foaming
   d. Always add water to a disinfectant to prevent foaming
   e. Always use hot water when mixing with disinfectants
   f. Disinfectant solutions should be replaced at least once a day
101. Since tool handles do not usually come in contact with clients and disinfectants may be hard on the skin, tool handles do not need to be immersed in disinfectant during the disinfection process.
   a. True
   b. False
102. You should not service clients with nails that have Leukonychia spots or white spots since Leukonychia spots indicate a nail infection.
   a. True
   b. False
103. Proper hand-washing requires which of the following? Select all that apply.
   a. Liquid soap
   b. Running water
   c. Nail brush
   d. Clean towel
104. Items should be disinfected before they are cleaned.
   a. True
   b. False
105. Fungal infections are more common in the
   a. Hands
   b. Feet
106. _____ are a set of infection control practices used to prevent transmission of diseases that can be acquired by contact with blood, body fluids, non-intact skin (including rashes), and mucous membranes.
   a. Disease control
   b. Standard cautions
   c. Standard precautions
   d. None of the above.
107. Which UV gel is used to enhance the thickness of other gels and provide a smoother surface?
   a. UV bonding gels
   b. UV building gels
   c. UV self leveling gels
   d. UV gel polishes

108. Cleaning the screen and other removable parts of a foot spa with chelating detergent should be done
    a. After every client use
    b. At the end of every day
    c. At least once a week
    d. At least once a month

109. Cutting or removing hardened tissue, such as calluses, is considered a medical procedure.
    a. True
    b. False

110. Which of the following can live for weeks on surfaces, but require a host (human or animal) to grow or multiply?
    a. Bacteria
    b. Fungi
    c. Parasite
    d. Virus

# Practice Exam 3

1. Which nail file grit is best for toenails?
   a. Fine
   b. Small
   c. Medium
   d. Large
2. Signs of a skin infection include? Select all that apply.
   a. Pus
   b. Pimple or abscess
   c. Inflammation
   d. Swelling
   e. Skin that appears white
   f. Skin that feels hot
   g. Skin that feels cold
3. Most disinfectants do not destroy spores.
   a. True
   b. False
4. Which muscles are used to separate the fingers?
   a. Pronators
   b. Supinators
   c. Abductors
   d. Adductors
5. Nail polishes contain _____ which help keep it flexible.
   a. UV stabilizers
   b. Acrylics
   c. Adhesives
   d. Plasticizers
6. The SDS Regulatory Information category lists OSHA's permissible exposure limits.
   a. True
   b. False
7. Which of the following is created by a chemical reaction? Select all that apply.
   a. Nail polish coatings
   b. Nail enhancements
   c. UV gel coatings
   d. None of the above
8. What are the functions of the skin? Select all that apply.
   a. Protection
   b. Sensation
   c. Heat regulation
   d. Excretion
   e. Secretion
9. The live tissue attached to the nail plate is called the:
   a. Cuticle

b. Eponychium

10. Thermal initiators get energy when exposed to UV.
    a. True
    b. False

11. Nail polish should be shaken often to ensure an even polish consistency.
    a. True
    b. False

12. Which tool can be used to reduce the sides of the free edge to reduce chances of an ingrown nail?
    a. Toenail clippers
    b. Nail rasp
    c. Foot files or pedicure paddles
    d. Nail files

13. After cleaning implements, implements should be dried before being immersed in disinfectant solution.
    a. True
    b. False

14. Bone and cartilage are examples of what type of tissue?
    a. Adipose
    b. Connective
    c. Epithelial
    d. Muscle
    e. Nerve

15. Before applying nail polish, you should ask clients to put on any jewelry or outerwear they took off before service.
    a. True
    b. False

16. Nail wraps are a type of
    a. Nail tip
    b. Overlay
    c. Nail resin
    d. Nail adhesive

17. Applying nail enhancement products over wet nail primers can cause the nail enhancement product to discolor and break down.
    a. True
    b. False

18. With proper home maintenance, how long should a nail polish application last?
    a. 3 to 5 days
    b. 7 to 10 days
    c. 14 to 21 days
    d. 21 to 31 days

19. What type of information should be recorded after completing a procedure? Select all that apply.
    a. Products used

b. Observations

c. Products recommended

d. Services performed

20. Which of the following is performed during post-service procedures? Select all that apply.

    a. Promoting products

    b. Scheduling the next appointment

    c. Thanking the client

    d. Disinfecting implements

    e. Reset the work area

21. Which UV gel is used to enhance the thickness of other gels and provide a smoother surface?

    a. UV bonding gels

    b. UV building gels

    c. UV self leveling gels

    d. UV gel polishes

22. Muscle tissue can be stimulated by which of the following? Select all that apply.

    a. Massage

    b. Electrical current

    c. Infrared light

    d. Dry or moist heat

    e. Nerve impulses

23. After service, a dappen dish should be cleaned with

    a. Alcohol

    b. Acetone

    c. Hot water

    d. A lint free towel

24. Which bits can be used in the cuticle area? Select all that apply.

    a. Cuticle safety bits

    b. Cone shaped bits

    c. Football shaped bits

    d. Bullet bits

    e. Small and large barrel bits

25. The amount of UV light produced by UV lamps is called UV light

    a. Viscosity

    b. Opacity

    c. Intensity

    d. Power

26. Nail primer should be applied to plastic nail tips to improve adhesion to the natural nail.

    a. True

    b. False

27. What are the advantages of gel polish?

    a. They are easier to remove than regular nail polish

    b. They do not smudge

c. They do not thicken over time

d. B and C

28. What is the first step in performing a manicure?

a. Shape the nails

b. Soften the cuticles

c. Clean under free edge

d. Remove old polish

29. Less pressure should be used when filing UV and LED gel enhancements than monomer and polymer enhancements.

a. True

b. False

30. The advantages of pre beveled nail tips include

a. Requiring less filing of the natural nail

b. Lessens potential damage to the natural nail

c. A and b

d. None of the above

31. What should be used to remove oil from nails?

a. A lint free towel

b. A nail activator

c. Acetone

d. A nail dehydrator

32. Which of the following is composed of specialized tissues that perform specific functions?

a. Cells

b. Nails

c. Hair

d. Stomach

33. The point where the nail tip is adhered to the natural nail is called the _____.

a. Position stop

b. Tip point

c. Well

d. Demarcation line

34. When removing the inhibition layer from the UV gel,

a. Wipe from the free edge of the fingernail towards the cuticle

b. Wipe from the cuticle towards the free edge of the fingernail

35. What should be applied to a split in the nail before wrapping it?

a. Top coat

b. Base coat

c. Adhesive glue

d. Nail hardener

36. _____ destroys or inactivates both the bacteria and viruses on hard, nonporous surfaces, but does not destroy bacterial spores.

a. Cleaning

b. Sanitizing

c. Disinfecting
d. Sterilizing
e. All of the above

37. When blending the nail tip at the contact area, the file should be held
    a. At a 30 degree angle
    b. At a 45 degree angle
    c. At a 90 degree angle
    d. Flat to the nail

38. What is used as a guide to extend the nail enhancement beyond the fingertip?
    a. Nail form
    b. A ruler
    c. Metal pusher
    d. Wooden pusher

39. Diseases that can spread from one person to person are considered
    a. Contagious
    b. Social
    c. Widespread
    d. Systemic

40. Free edge separation from nail enhancement products can be caused by ? Select all that apply.
    a. Nail enhancement product breakdown
    b. Aging of the nail enhancement product
    c. A client being hard on the nails
    d. Only A and B

41. A nail unit consists of which of the following? Select all that apply.
    a. Nail plate
    b. Nail bed
    c. Matrix
    d. Cuticle
    e. Eponychium
    f. Hyponychium
    g. Nail folds

42. During UV and LED gel maintenance, UV gel should be applied
    a. Only on the area of regrowth
    b. To the entire nail

43. When working with electric files with higher torque, you should work at _____ speeds.
    a. Higher
    b. Lower

44. Select all the true statements about a basic pedicure.
    a. Basic pedicures typically take 30 to 45 minutes
    b. Basic pedicures typically take 1 to 1.5 hours
    c. Basic pedicures include a foot massage
    d. Basic pedicures include a leg massage

45. Nail implements should be removed from their containers using _____ to prevent contamination.
    a. Two fingers
    b. Single use plastic or metal spatula
    c. Paper towels
    d. Cloth towel
46. The bottom of the foot is the only place a friction movement is used in a manicure and pedicure service.
    a. True
    b. False
47. The practice of _____ involves using essential oils to relax or invigorate the client.
    a. Reflexology
    b. Aromatherapy
    c. Dermatology
    d. Psychotherapy
48. The manicure service cushion should be _____throughout the service.
    a. Covered with a towel
    b. Covered with plastic
    c. Uncovered
49. If a client decides to get a paraffin wax treatment before a manicure, soaking the hands in water is not necessary because the paraffin treatment already softens the skin.
    a. True
    b. False
50. What bone is located in the thigh?
    a. Tibia
    b. Fibula
    c. Patella
    d. Femur
    e. Talus
51. Examples of conditions that require a series pedicure include? Select all that apply.
    a. Fungus nails
    b. Callus reduction
    c. Scaly feet
    d. Ingrown nails
52. In a massage technique called _____, the hands glide over a body part.
    a. Effleurage
    b. Petrissage
    c. Tapotement
    d. Vibration
53. Which nail shape is thought to be attractive on most women's hands?
    a. Square
    b. Squoval
    c. Round
    d. Oval

e. Pointed

54. What body system is responsible for fighting disease?
    a. Lymphatic
    b. Endocrine
    c. Integumentary
    d. Excretory

55. Products that are put into the water in a pedicure bath to soften the skin on the feet are called ?
    a. Foot soaks
    b. Foot scrubs
    c. Foot lotions
    d. Callus removers

56. Hot stones are typically made of
    a. Salt
    b. Basalt
    c. Granite
    d. Marble

57. Porous items that have been exposed to broken skin, blood, or body fluids must be thrown away.
    a. True
    b. False

58. Paraffin wax treatments should be avoided for? Select all that apply.
    a. Clients with impaired circulation
    b. Clients cuts or burns
    c. Clients with rashes or eczema
    d. Clients with warts

59. It is the responsibility of _____ to ensure proper infection control procedures are followed.
    a. Nail technician
    b. Salon
    c. Client
    d. Nail technician and salon

60. For ergonomic reasons, a nail technician's pedicuring stool should be
    a. High
    b. Low

61. For which one of the following are oil manicures recommended?
    a. Leukonychia
    b. Split nails
    c. Brittle nails
    d. Prevention of infection

62. Nails should be soaked in water before filing.
    a. True
    b. False

63. The process to clean both hands with a nail brush should take
    a. 15 seconds

      b. 20 seconds

      c. 30 seconds

      d. 60 seconds

64. The first step in cleaning and disinfecting implements in preparation for service is to put on gloves.

      a. True

      b. False

65. The _____ is a long bone found in the forearm that stretches from the elbow to the smallest finger.

      a. Humerus

      b. Ulna

      c. Radius

      d. Carpus

66. When working with nail nippers, the _____ should be placed on the box joint to help control the blade.

      a. Thumb

      b. Index finger

      c. Middle finger

      d. Index and middle finger

67. When using a metal pusher, the _____ should be held at a _____ angle. The _____ should be used to push back the dead cuticle tissue.

      a. Flat end, 20 to 30 degree, spoon end

      b. Flat end, 90 degree, spoon end

      c. Spoon end, 20 to 30 degree, flat end

      d. Spoon end, 90 degree, flat end

68. Which of the following instruments are used to remove dead cuticle tissue from the nail plate? Select all that apply.

      a. Metal pusher

      b. Wooden pusher

      c. Nail nipper

      d. Tweezer

      e. Nail clipper

69. Improper curing of UV or LED gel can lead to? Select all that apply.

      a. Skin cancer

      b. Service breakdown

      c. Skin irritation

      d. Skin sensitivity

70. Which of the following are single-use implements. Select all that apply.

      a. Metal pushers

      b. Nail clippers

      c. Tweezers

      d. Nail nippers

      e. None of the above.

71. Nail technicians should have at least ___ set of stainless steel implements to have a clean and disinfected set ready for each client.
    a. One
    b. Two
    c. Three
    d. Five
72. A lower grit abrasive file and buffer should be used to file and polish natural nails.
    a. True
    b. False
73. How should implements be immersed in disinfection containers? Select all that apply.
    a. Immerse only parts of the implements that come into contact with clients
    b. Immerse all implements completely, except for the handles so that you can remove the implements without coming into contact with the disinfectant
    c. Immerse all implements completely
    d. All disinfectant containers must have lids to prevent the disinfectant solution from being contaminated.
74. Wooden pushers can be used to? Select all that apply.
    a. Remove dead cuticle tissue
    b. Clean under the free edge of nails
    c. Cut the nails
    d. Apply products
75. _____ is the study of the functions of a body's structures.
    a. Anatomy
    b. Physiology
    c. Biology
    d. Histology
76. The surface of a standard manicuring table should
    a. Be made of a soft material, for the client's comfort
    b. Be made of wood
    c. Be made of a hard and impenetrable surface
77. Which of the following are true statements? Select all that apply.
    a. The nail technician's chair should not have wheels.
    b. The client's chair should not have wheels.
    c. The client's chair should have no or low arms on the sides.
    d. None of the above
78. Both the HIV and Hepatitis virus can live on surfaces outside the body for long periods of time.
    a. True
    b. False
79. What information should be included in a client intake form? Select all that apply.
    a. Medical history
    b. Client contact information
    c. Past nail service history
    d. Sexual orientation

e. Nail appointment goals

80. Massaging the legs that suffer from varicose veins may be harmful to the client because it increases circulation.
    a. True
    b. False

81. How much time should you allot for a client consultation?
    a. 2 to 5 minutes
    b. 5 to 15 minutes
    c. 15 to 30 minutes
    d. 30 minutes to 1 hour

82. _____ increase the rate at which chemical reactions occur.
    a. Thermal initiators
    b. Photoinitiators
    c. Catalysts
    d. Oligomers

83. Methacrylates, acrylates, and cyanoacrylates are examples of
    a. Catalysts
    b. Acrylics
    c. Solvents
    d. Initiators

84. Nail enhancements can further harden during the first 48 hours.
    a. True
    b. False

85. Another word for curing is _____.
    a. Evaporation
    b. Preservation
    c. Scarification
    d. Polymerization

86. Soak the nail plate in _____ to soften the nail plate. Select all that apply.
    a. Primer
    b. Acetone
    c. Remover solvent
    d. None of the above

87. A _____ change is a change in the composition of a substance or the creation of a new substance.
    a. Physical
    b. Chemical

88. _____ soften nail cuticles and calluses.
    a. Acids
    b. Alkalis

89. Which of the following is an example of an adhesive?
    a. Nail primer
    b. Nail dehydrator
    c. Top coats

d. All of the above

90. Repeated pressure on an area of the skin can cause it to develop into
    a. A bolus
    b. A wart
    c. A callus
    d. An infection

91. What is the actively growing part of the nail?
    a. Lunula
    b. Matrix
    c. Mantle
    d. Free edge

92. Clients with nail fungus infections should not be serviced.
    a. True
    b. False

93. Nail polish is applied to the
    a. Nail bed
    b. Nail plate
    c. Eponychium
    d. Hyponychium

94. Eczema and psoriasis are not contagious.
    a. True
    b. False

95. The primary functions of the skeletal system are? Select all that apply.
    a. Support the body
    b. Protect internal organs
    c. Help produce red and white blood cells
    d. Store most of the body's calcium supply
    e. Blood and nutrient circulation

96. _____ are the basic units of all living things.
    a. Cells
    b. Tissues
    c. Organs
    d. Protoplasm

97. A client contracts a skin infection after being accidentally cut with contaminated nail clippers. This is considered _____ transmission.
    a. Direct
    b. Indirect

98. _____ are used to break down hard to remove residues of pedicure products, especially areas with hard tap water.
    a. Antibacterial soaps
    b. Antimicrobial soaps
    c. Fungicidal soaps
    d. Chelating soaps
    e. None of the above

99. You can service a client's hands or feet that show signs of infection as long as you disinfect your tools before and after servicing the client.
    a. True
    b. False

100. Which of the following is highly resistant to antibiotics?
    a. Streptococci
    b. Bacilli
    c. Spirilla
    d. MRSA

101. Which of the following categories is/are NOT found in the SDS? Select all that apply.
    a. Hazard Identification
    b. First-aid Measures
    c. Fire-fighting Measures
    d. Expiration Information
    e. Regulatory Information

102. A _____ is the point where two or more bones meet.
    a. Cartilage
    b. Joint
    c. Tendon
    d. None of the above

103. Salons must use disinfectants that are approved by:
    a. Environmental Protection Agency
    b. Food and Drug Administration
    c. Center for Disease Control
    d. None of the above

104. All porous items are single-use only.
    a. True
    b. False

105. Clients must wash their hands before you begin service.
    a. True
    b. False

106. Which of the following is a chemical process? Select all that apply.
    a. Cleaning
    b. Sanitizing
    c. Disinfecting
    d. None of the above.

107. The two steps of proper infection control are:
    a. Cleaning and sterilizing
    b. Cleaning and disinfecting
    c. Sterilizing and disinfecting

108. Hard and soft UV gels can both be removed using acetone
    a. True
    b. False

109. The best time to recommend retail products to clients is

a. During pre-service procedures
b. During the procedure
c. During post-service procedures
110. When cleaning and disinfecting foot spas or basins, the basin
a. Should be allowed to air dry
b. Should be wiped dry with linen
c. Should be wiped dry with paper towels

# Section 2

# Infection Control and Safety Practices

1. Which of the following are reusable items? Select all that apply.
   a. Towels
   b. Bits
   c. Pumice stone
   d. Some buffers
   e. Wooden sticks

2. As part of the SDS categories, Disposal Consideration includes proper disposal and
   a. Chemical hazards
   b. Disposal restrictions
   c. Restrictions on transportation
   d. All of the above

3. An antiseptic is used in manicuring to
   a. bleach the nails
   b. treat minor cuts
   c. smooth corrugated nails
   d. give the nails a high sheen

4. Hands should be washed a minimum of
   a. 10 seconds
   b. 15 seconds
   c. 20 seconds
   d. 30 seconds

5. When cleaning and disinfecting pipeless foot spas, the impeller, footplate, and any other removable components must be removed, cleaned, and disinfected after every client.
   a. True
   b. False

6. A _____ is used to keep a record of equipment usage, cleaning, and disinfecting.
   a. Notebook
   b. Spreadsheet
   c. Filing system
   d. Logbook

7. Which type of hepatitis are you most likely to encounter at a salon?
   a. Hepatitis A
   b. Hepatitis B
   c. Hepatitis C
   d. B & C

8. Soaking foot spas and basins in disinfectant overnight should be done
   a. At least once a week
   b. At least twice a week
   c. At least once every 2 weeks
   d. At least once a month

9. Hinged instruments should be in the _____ position before being immersed in disinfectant solution.

a. Open

b. Closed

10. A(n) _____ is when an employee comes into contact with potentially infectious material.

    a. Accident

    b. Emergency

    c. Exposure incident

    d. Hazmat exposure

11. Standard precautions involve which of the following? Select all that apply.

    a. Washing hands

    b. Wearing gloves when there is a potential for blood exposure

    c. Proper disposal of sharp instruments

    d. Proper disposal of items contaminated with blood and/or body fluids

    e. Wearing masks when there is a potential for exposure to airborne pathogens

12. Hand sanitizers or antiseptics can be used in place of hand washing.

    a. True

    b. False

13. If a client brings in their own tools and implements, you must disinfect their tools and implements before using them on the client.

    a. True

    b. False

14. Porous items that have been exposed to broken skin, blood, or body fluids must be thrown away.

    a. True

    b. False

15. Which bacteria is most likely to cause diseases such as pneumonia?

    a. Staphylococci

    b. Streptococci

    c. Diplococci

    d. Bacilli

    e. Spirilla

16. Multi-use items that have been exposed to blood or body fluids must be thrown away.

    a. True

    b. False

17. Which of the following statements is NOT true? Select all that apply.

    a. Always wear gloves and safety glasses when mixing disinfectants.

    b. Always use tongs or gloves to remove items from disinfectants

    c. Always add a disinfectant to water to prevent foaming

    d. Always add water to a disinfectant to prevent foaming

    e. Always use hot water when mixing with disinfectants

    f. Disinfectant solutions should be replaced at least once a day

18. Which of the following should NOT be used to disinfect pedicure tubs?

    a. Quats

    b. Phenolics

    c. Bleach

d. None of the above

19. Unless otherwise specified by the manufacturer, a disinfectant contact time of ____ minutes is required for all items.
    a. 5
    b. 10
    c. 15
    d. 20

20. Since tool handles do not usually come in contact with clients and disinfectants may be hard on the skin, tool handles do not need to be immersed in disinfectant during the disinfection process.
    a. True
    b. False

21. The SDS Regulatory Information category lists OSHA's permissible exposure limits.
    a. True
    b. False

22. Proper hand-washing requires which of the following? Select all that apply.
    a. Liquid soap
    b. Running water
    c. Nail brush
    d. Clean towel

23. Items should be disinfected before they are cleaned.
    a. True
    b. False

24. Fungal infections are more common in the
    a. Hands
    b. Feet

25. _____ are a set of infection control practices used to prevent transmission of diseases that can be acquired by contact with blood, body fluids, non-intact skin (including rashes), and mucous membranes.
    a. Disease control
    b. Standard cautions
    c. Standard precautions
    d. None of the above.

26. Which type of hepatitis virus is most difficult to kill on a surface?
    a. Hepatitis A
    b. Hepatitis B
    c. Hepatitis C
    d. A & B

27. Cleaning the screen and other removable parts of a foot spa with chelating detergent should be done
    a. After every client use
    b. At the end of every day
    c. At least once a week
    d. At least once a month

28. Cutting or removing hardened tissue, such as calluses, is considered a medical procedure.
    a. True
    b. False
29. Select all statements that are true.
    a. Warts are highly contagious parasites.
    b. Warts are highly contagious viruses.
    c. Warts are most commonly found on the bottom of the feet or on the fingers or palms.
    d. None of the above.
30. Which of the following can live for weeks on surfaces, but require a host (human or animal) to grow or multiply?
    a. Bacteria
    b. Fungi
    c. Parasite
    d. Virus
31. A client contracts a skin infection after being accidentally cut with contaminated nail clippers. This is considered _____ transmission.
    a. Direct
    b. Indirect
32. Most disinfectants do not destroy spores.
    a. True
    b. False
33. _____ are used to break down hard to remove residues of pedicure products, especially areas with hard tap water.
    a. Antibacterial soaps
    b. Antimicrobial soaps
    c. Fungicidal soaps
    d. Chelating soaps
    e. None of the above
34. Diseases that can spread from one person to person are considered
    a. Contagious
    b. Social
    c. Widespread
    d. Systemic
35. You can service a client's hands or feet that show signs of infection as long as you disinfect your tools before and after servicing the client.
    a. True
    b. False
36. Signs of a skin infection include? Select all that apply.
    a. Pus
    b. Pimple or abscess
    c. Inflammation
    d. Swelling

e. Skin that appears white

f. Skin that feels hot

g. Skin that feels cold

37. Which of the following is highly resistant to antibiotics?

    a. Streptococci

    b. Bacilli

    c. Spirilla

    d. MRSA

38. Which of the following categories is/are NOT found in the SDS? Select all that apply.

    a. Hazard Identification

    b. First-aid Measures

    c. Fire-fighting Measures

    d. Expiration Information

    e. Regulatory Information

39. Salons must use disinfectants that are approved by:

    a. Environmental Protection Agency

    b. Food and Drug Administration

    c. Center for Disease Control

    d. None of the above

40. After cleaning implements, implements should be dried before being immersed in disinfectant solution.

    a. True

    b. False

41. All porous items are single-use only.

    a. True

    b. False

42. Which of the following is a chemical process? Select all that apply.

    a. Cleaning

    b. Sanitizing

    c. Disinfecting

    d. None of the above.

43. _____ destroys or inactivates both the bacteria and viruses on hard, nonporous surfaces, but does not destroy bacterial spores.

    a. Cleaning

    b. Sanitizing

    c. Disinfecting

    d. Sterilizing

    e. All of the above.

44. Both the HIV and Hepatitis virus can live on surfaces outside the body for long periods of time.

    a. True

    b. False

45. The two steps of proper infection control are:

    a. Cleaning and sterilizing

b. Cleaning and disinfecting

c. Sterilizing and disinfecting

46. When cleaning and disinfecting foot spas or basins, the basin

    a. Should be allowed to air dry

    b. Should be wiped dry with linen

    c. Should be wiped dry with paper towels

# Human Anatomy and Physiology

1. Which muscles are used to form a straight line with the wrist, hand, and fingers?
    a. Extensors
    b. Flexors
    c. Pronators
    d. Supinator
2. What is responsible for skin pigment?
    a. Elastin
    b. Keratin
    c. Collagen
    d. Melanocytes
3. Common places for skin allergies to occur include which of the following? Select all that apply.
    a. Between a nail technician's thumb and pointer finger
    b. On a nail technician's wrist, palm, or back of the hand
    c. On a nail technician's face
    d. On a client's eponychium, fingertips, or nail bed
4. Nerves and blood vessels are found in the nail
    a. Bed
    b. Wall
    c. Plate
    d. Grooves
5. What are the group of five bones of the hand between the wrist and the fingers?
    a. Carpus
    b. Metacarpus
    c. Phalanges
    d. None of the above
6. Which one of the following is a condition in which the cuticle splits around the nail?
    a. Hangnails
    b. Pterygium
    c. Onychophagy
    d. Onychorrhexis
7. Which muscles help bend the foot down? Select all that apply.
    a. Extensor digitorum longus
    b. Tibialis anterior
    c. Peroneus brevis
    d. Soleus
8. Ingrown nails are also known as
    a. Onychia
    b. Onychocryptosis
    c. Onychomadesis
    d. Onychomycosis
9. Contact dermatitis is an avoidable skin disease.

a. True
b. False

10. Which of the following can lead to improper curing of UV gels? Select all that apply.
    a. Applying products too thickly
    b. Not enough time under the UV lamp
    c. Dirty UV lamps
    d. Using a UV lamp not specifically designated for the UV gel system

11. The nail plate is non porous.
    a. True
    b. False

12. Which of the following muscle types are under voluntary control? Select all that apply.
    a. Smooth
    b. Striated
    c. Non-striated
    d. Cardiac

13. Complete replacement of a fingernail takes about
    a. 1 to 2 months
    b. 3 months
    c. 4 to 6 months
    d. 12 months

14. The white, half-mooned shape at the bottom of the nail plate is called
    a. The free edge
    b. The closed edge
    c. The open edge
    d. The lunula

15. Which nail condition is associated with brittle nails with lengthwise ridges?
    a. Beau's line
    b. Plicatured nail
    c. Eggshell nails
    d. Melanonychia
    e. Onychorrhexis

16. The skin is an example of what type of tissue?
    a. Adipose
    b. Connective
    c. Epithelial
    d. Muscle
    e. Nerve

17. Nail technicians are allowed to push back, as well as, cut the eponychium.
    a. True
    b. False

18. Damage to the _____ can change the shape and thickness of the nail plate.
    a. Hyponychium
    b. Eponychium
    c. Matrix

19. Damage to the hyponychium can cause which of the following?
    a. Separation between the nail plate and nail bed
    b. Increase risk of infection underneath the nail plate
    c. A and B
    d. None of the above
20. The live tissue attached to the nail plate is called the:
    a. Cuticle
    b. Eponychium
21. Nail plate cells are formed in the
    a. Nail bed
    b. Nail fold
    c. Matrix
    d. Free edge
22. Skin and nails are a part of which body system?
    a. Lymphatic
    b. Endocrine
    c. Integumentary
    d. Excretory
23. Which muscle is used to move the big toe?
    a. Flexor digiti minimi
    b. Flexor digitorum brevis
    c. Abductor hallucis
    d. Abductor digiti minimi
24. A 36 watt UV lamp unit will emit 36 watts of UV energy.
    a. True
    b. False
25. Contact dermatitis can be caused by which of the following? Select all that apply.
    a. Prolonged and repeated contact with substances
    b. Improper product consistency
    c. Undercuring UV or LED gel enhancements
    d. Exposure to allergy causing substances
26. Albinism is associated with _____.
    a. Chloasma
    b. Lentigines
    c. Leukoderma
    d. Nevus
27. You should not service clients with nails that have Leukonychia spots or white spots since Leukonychia spots indicate a nail infection.
    a. True
    b. False
28. A(n) _____ is a pooling of blood underneath the skin or nails.
    a. Keloid
    b. Hematoma
    c. Ulcer

    d.  Fissure

    e.  Excoriation

    f.  Scale

29. Hives are examples of what type of primary skin lesions?
   - a. Cyst
   - b. Macule
   - c. Vesicle
   - d. Wheal

30. What are the functions of the skin? Select all that apply.
   - a. Protection
   - b. Sensation
   - c. Heat regulation
   - d. Excretion
   - e. Secretion

31. Acne is usually the result of a blocked _____.
   - a. Sudoriferous gland
   - b. Sebaceous gland
   - c. Nerve
   - d. None of the above

32. The foot is composed of which of the following? Select all that apply.
   - a. Carpus
   - b. Tarsals
   - c. Metacarpus
   - d. Metatarsals
   - e. Phalanges

33. What layer of the skin is fat tissue found in?
   - a. Epidermis
   - b. Dermis
   - c. Subcutaneous

34. The _____ contains no blood vessels.
   - a. Dermis
   - b. Epidermis

35. Repeated pressure on an area of the skin can cause it to develop into
   - a. A bolus
   - b. A wart
   - c. A callus
   - d. An infection

36. A nail unit consists of which of the following? Select all that apply.
   - a. Nail plate
   - b. Nail bed
   - c. Matrix
   - d. Cuticle
   - e. Eponychium
   - f. Hyponychium

g.  Nail folds

37. Which muscles are used to separate the fingers?
    a.  Pronators
    b.  Supinators
    c.  Abductors
    d.  Adductors

38. What is the actively growing part of the nail?
    a.  Lunula
    b.  Matrix
    c.  Mantle
    d.  Free edge

39. Muscle tissue can be stimulated by which of the following? Select all that apply.
    a.  Massage
    b.  Electrical current
    c.  Infrared light
    d.  Dry or moist heat
    e.  Nerve impulses

40. Clients with nail fungus infections should not be serviced.
    a.  True
    b.  False

41. Nail polish is applied to the
    a.  Nail bed
    b.  Nail plate
    c.  Eponychium
    d.  Hyponychium

42. What bone is located in the thigh?
    a.  Tibia
    b.  Fibula
    c.  Patella
    d.  Femur
    e.  Talus

43. Eczema and psoriasis are not contagious.
    a.  True
    b.  False

44. The _____ is a long bone found in the forearm that stretches from the elbow to the smallest finger.
    a.  Humerus
    b.  Ulna
    c.  Radius
    d.  Carpus

45. A _____ is the point where two or more bones meet.
    a.  Cartilage
    b.  Joint
    c.  Tendon

d. None of the above

46. The primary functions of the skeletal system are? Select all that apply.
    a. Support the body
    b. Protect internal organs
    c. Help produce red and white blood cells
    d. Store most of the body's calcium supply
    e. Blood and nutrient circulation

47. What body system is responsible for fighting disease?
    a. Lymphatic
    b. Endocrine
    c. Integumentary
    d. Excretory

48. Which of the following is composed of specialized tissues that perform specific functions?
    a. Cells
    b. Nails
    c. Hair
    d. Stomach

49. Bone and cartilage are examples of what type of tissue?
    a. Adipose
    b. Connective
    c. Epithelial
    d. Muscle
    e. Nerve

50. _____ are the basic units of all living things.
    a. Cells
    b. Tissues
    c. Organs
    d. Protoplasm

51. _____ is the study of the functions of a body's structures.
    a. Anatomy
    b. Physiology
    c. Biology
    d. Histology

# Chemistry of Nail Products

1. Liquid soaps can neutralize callus softeners.
    a. True
    b. False
2. N95 masks are effective against vapors.
    a. True
    b. False
3. Colored polymer powders are an example of
    a. A pure substance
    b. A physical mixture
    c. A suspension
    d. None of the above
4. Which of the following is used in nail polish dryers and skin protectants?
    a. Silicone
    b. Glycerin
    c. VOCs
    d. All of the above
5. Which of the following uses thermal initiators?
    a. UV curing products
    b. Monomer liquid systems
    c. Polymer powder systems
    d. B and C
    e. All of the above
6. Volatile organic compounds (VOCs) can be found in ? Select all that apply
    a. Nail polish
    b. Polish removers
    c. Base and top coats
    d. None of the above
7. Water is a _____.
    a. Solution
    b. Solute
    c. Solvent
    d. All of the above.
8. Nail polish is an example of:
    a. An emulsion
    b. A surfactant
    c. A suspension
    d. All of the above
9. A _____ change is a change in the form of a substance.
    a. Physical
    b. Chemical
10. A 2 inch thick bed of activated carbon filter can properly absorb vapors and remove them from the salon air.

a. True
b. False

11. Sodium hydroxide or lye is an
    a. Acid
    b. Alkali

12. You should recommend nail penetrating oils to clients to keep natural and enhanced nails moisturized and flexible.
    a. True
    b. False

13. Acetone is inflammable.
    a. True
    b. False

14. When nail problems occur, they are most likely due to ?
    a. Improper nail plate preparation
    b. Improper application or maintenance of nail products
    c. Improper removal of nail products
    d. All of the above

15. Thermal initiators get energy when exposed to UV.
    a. True
    b. False

16. Products made from _____ are harder to dissolve.
    a. Non cross-linked polymers
    b. Cross-linked polymers

17. Nail polishes contain _____ which prevent fading and discoloration from sunlight.
    a. Acrylics
    b. Adhesives
    c. UV stabilizers
    d. Plasticizers

18. Select all the reasons why Methyl methacrylate monomer (MMA) should not be used in nail salons.
    a. MMA is toxic.
    b. MMA nail products do not adhere well to the nail plate unless the nail plate has been shredded.
    c. MMA creates nails that are hard and difficult to break.
    d. MMA is very difficult to remove.
    e. The FDA says not to use it.

19. Water and oil are examples of _____ liquids.
    a. Miscible
    b. Immiscible

20. Which of the following is used as a solvent as well as a moisturizer?
    a. Silicone
    b. Glycerin
    c. VOCs
    d. All of the above

21. All nail enhancements and nail adhesives are made from acrylics.
    a. True
    b. False
22. What is responsible for UV gels thick and sticky consistency and ability to harden quickly?
    a. Oligomers
    b. Polymers
    c. Methyl methacrylate monomer
    d. None of the above
23. _____ increase the rate at which chemical reactions occur.
    a. Thermal initiators
    b. Photoinitiators
    c. Catalysts
    d. Oligomers
24. Methacrylates, acrylates, and cyanoacrylates are examples of
    a. Catalysts
    b. Acrylics
    c. Solvents
    d. Initiators
25. Nail enhancements can further harden during the first 48 hours.
    a. True
    b. False
26. Another word for curing is _____.
    a. Evaporation
    b. Preservation
    c. Scarification
    d. Polymerization
27. Soak the nail plate in _____ to soften the nail plate. Select all that apply.
    a. Primer
    b. Acetone
    c. Remover solvent
    d. None of the above
28. A _____ change is a change in the composition of a substance or the creation of a new substance.
    a. Physical
    b. Chemical
29. Which of the following is created by a chemical reaction? Select all that apply.
    a. Nail polish coatings
    b. Nail enhancements
    c. UV gel coatings
    d. None of the above
30. _____ soften nail cuticles and calluses.
    a. Acids
    b. Alkalis

31. Nail polishes contain _____ which help keep it flexible.
- a. UV stabilizers
- b. Acrylics
- c. Adhesives
- d. Plasticizers

32. Which of the following is an example of an adhesive?
- a. Nail primer
- b. Nail dehydrator
- c. Top coats
- d. All of the above

# Client Consultation and Documentation

1. When dealing with a dissatisfied client, you should
   a. Try to make the client happy, at all cost
   b. Inform the client on why you are right
   c. Try to make the client happy, within reason
   d. Immediately ask them to speak to the salon manager
2. Which of the following should you do during the client consultation? Select all that apply.
   a. Review the client intake form.
   b. Assess your client's hands and nails
   c. Ask about your client's career
   d. Ask about your client's hobbies
   e. Upsell services
3. When meeting an older client for the first time, you should
   a. Address them by their first name
   b. Address them by the honorific (e.g. "Mrs"/"Mr")
   c. Address them as "Sir" or "M'am"
   d. Asked them how they'd like to be addressed
4. How should you deal with tardy clients? Select all that apply.
   a. Follow the salons appointment policies
   b. If you client is late, but you can fit them in without jeopardizing other appointments, let the client know even though they are late, you will still able to service them
   c. If the client is frequently late for their appointments, schedule their appointment for the end of the day or tell them to arrive earlier than their actual appointment time
5. When dealing with a scheduling mix-up, you should
   a. Try to determine who is at fault to see who is responsible for fixing the mix-up
   b. Do not worry about who is at fault and work on resolving the situation
   c. Ignore the mix-up and try to squeeze the client into the schedule
6. Foot and leg massages are contraindicated in patients with which of the following? Select all that apply.
   a. Diabetes
   b. Hypertension
   c. Varicose veins
   d. Hay fever
7. Extra precaution should be taken when working with clients that have which of the following conditions? Select all that apply.
   a. Arthritis
   b. Circulatory diseases
   c. Diabetes
   d. High blood pressure
8. What information should be included in a client intake form? Select all that apply.
   a. Medical history

b. Client contact information
c. Past nail service history
d. Sexual orientation
e. Nail appointment goals

9. Massaging the legs that suffer from varicose veins may be harmful to the client because it increases circulation.
    a. True
    b. False

10. How much time should you allot for a client consultation?
    a. 2 to 5 minutes
    b. 5 to 15 minutes
    c. 15 to 30 minutes
    d. 30 minutes to 1 hour

# Nail Service Tools

1. Pumice stone is used in pedicuring as
   a. an abrasive
   b. a bleach
   c. a lubricant
   d. an astringent

2. Which abrasive is used to shorten and shape natural nails?
   a. A lower grit abrasive
   b. A medium grit abrasive
   c. A higher grit abrasive
   d. A fine grit abrasive

3. What product should be applied to brittle nails to help strengthen the nail?
   a. Protein hardeners
   b. Methylene glycol hardeners
   c. Dimethylurea hardeners
   d. B and C

4. What should be applied to nails to prevent natural nail discoloration or yellowish discoloration of nail polish?
   a. Nail oils
   b. Nail hardener
   c. Base coat
   d. Top coat

5. Excessive use of cuticle removers can lead to
   a. Dry skin
   b. Dry eponychium
   c. Hangnails
   d. A and B
   e. A,B, and C

6. Which product is designed to be absorbed into nails to make them more flexible?
   a. Nail creams
   b. Nail oils
   c. Nail polish remover
   d. Nail soap

7. Which of the following are true statements? Select all that apply.
   a. Gloves must be worn when servicing a client.
   b. A new set of gloves must be used for each client.
   c. If performing both a manicure and pedicure for a single client, a new set of gloves must be worn for each service.
   d. Hands should be washed or antimicrobial gel should be applied after removing gloves and before putting on new gloves.

8. Acetone based polish removers dissolve polish quicker than non-acetone based polish removers.
   a. True

b. False
9. When using two-way or three-way buffers, start with the lowest grit surface.
   a. True
   b. False
10. Fine grit abrasives have
    a. Grits of 180 or lower
    b. Grits of 180
    c. Grits between 180 and 240
    d. Grits of 240 or higher
11. The process of preparing a nail file for use by using another clean file to rub away sharp edges is called
    a. Abrasive conditioning
    b. File prepping
    c. File polishing
    d. None of the above
12. What product should be used to prevent nail polish from chipping?
    a. Nail oils
    b. Nail hardener
    c. Base coat
    d. Top coat
13. Which of the following statements is true?
    a. The lower the grit, the larger the abrasive particles; make the file less abrasive.
    b. The lower the grit, the larger the abrasive particles; making the file more abrasive.
    c. The lower the grit, the smaller the abrasive particles; making the file less abrasive.
    d. The lower the grit, the smaller the abrasive particles; making the file more abrasive.
14. Nail files and buffers are considered multi-use items.
    a. True
    b. False
15. Nail polish should be shaken often to ensure an even polish consistency.
    a. True
    b. False
16. Which of the following do not harbor or support microbial growth? Select all that apply.
    a. Nail polish
    b. Monomers
    c. Polymers
    d. UV gels
    e. Nail primers
    f. Nail oil
17. Bacteria on a nail polish brush can be transferred to another client's nails if the nail polish brush is immediately used.
    a. True

b. False

18. When working with nail nippers, the _____ should be placed on the box joint to help control the blade.
    a. Thumb
    b. Index finger
    c. Middle finger
    d. Index and middle finger

19. When using a metal pusher, the _____ should be held at a _____ angle. The _____ should be used to push back the dead cuticle tissue.
    a. Flat end, 20 to 30 degree, spoon end
    b. Flat end, 90 degree, spoon end
    c. Spoon end, 20 to 30 degree, flat end
    d. Spoon end, 90 degree, flat end

20. Which of the following instruments are used to remove dead cuticle tissue from the nail plate? Select all that apply.
    a. Metal pusher
    b. Wooden pusher
    c. Nail nipper
    d. Tweezer
    e. Nail clipper

21. Which of the following are single-use implements. Select all that apply.
    a. Metal pushers
    b. Nail clippers
    c. Tweezers
    d. Nail nippers
    e. None of the above.

22. Nail technicians should have at least ___ set of stainless steel implements to have a clean and disinfected set ready for each client.
    a. One
    b. Two
    c. Three
    d. Five

23. A lower grit abrasive file and buffer should be used to file and polish natural nails.
    a. True
    b. False

24. How should implements be immersed in disinfection containers? Select all that apply.
    a. Immerse only parts of the implements that come into contact with clients
    b. Immerse all implements completely, except for the handles so that you can remove the implements without coming into contact with the disinfectant
    c. Immerse all implements completely
    d. All disinfectant containers must have lids to prevent the disinfectant solution from being contaminated.

25. Wooden pushers can be used to? Select all that apply.
    a. Remove dead cuticle tissue

b. Clean under the free edge of nails

c. Cut the nails

d. Apply products

26. The surface of a standard manicuring table should

    a. Be made of a soft material, for the client's comfort

    b. Be made of wood

    c. Be made of a hard and impenetrable surface

27. Which of the following are true statements? Select all that apply.

    a. The nail technician's chair should not have wheels.

    b. The client's chair should not have wheels.

    c. The client's chair should have no or low arms on the sides.

    d. None of the above

# Nail Service Preparation

1. The manicure table should be cleaned and disinfected as part of the pre-service procedure.
   a. True
   b. False
2. A communal nail brush can be used by multiple clients to wash their hands.
   a. True
   b. False
3. Hands should be washed for a minimum of
   a. 15 seconds
   b. 20 seconds
   c. 30 seconds
   d. 60 seconds
4. Lamps attached to the manicuring table should use a fluorescent bulb or a _____ incandescent bulb.
   a. 20 to 40 watt
   b. 40 to 60 watt
   c. 60 to 80 watt
   d. 80 to 100 watt
5. The correct order of steps for cleaning and disinfecting implements are
   a. Put on gloves, soak implements in disinfectant, wash implements with soap, rinse implements with warm water and dry implements, store implements in a clean and dry container, remove gloves and wash your hands
   b. Put on gloves, wash implements with soap, rinse implements with warm water, soak implements in disinfectant, rinse and dry implements, remove gloves and wash your hands, store implements in a clean and dry container
   c. Wash implements with soap, rinse implements with warm water, put on gloves, soak implements in disinfectant, rinse and dry implements, store implements in a clean and dry container, remove gloves and wash your hands
   d. Put on gloves, wash implements with soap, rinse implements with warm water, soak implements in disinfectant, rinse and dry implements, store implements in a clean and dry container, remove gloves and wash your hands
6. Disinfected implements should be
   a. Left on an open shelf and allowed to air dry
   b. Stored in a clean and dry container until needed
   c. Wrapped in a towel and stored on an open shelf
7. After washing and drying your hands, you should use a towel (paper or cloth) to open the door.
   a. True
   b. False
8. The process to clean both hands with a nail brush should take
   a. 15 seconds
   b. 20 seconds

c. 30 seconds

d. 60 seconds

9. Clients must wash their hands before you begin service.

    a. True

    b. False

10. The first step in cleaning and disinfecting implements in preparation for service is to put on gloves.

    a. True

    b. False

# Manicure and Pedicure Services

1. After each use, manicuring implements should be
   a. wiped with a towel
   b. wiped with a tissue
   c. cleansed and disinfected
   d. placed in dry storage
2. Where should all manicuring cosmetic supplies be kept when not being used?
   a. On a clean shelf
   b. On the manicuring table
   c. In a clean manicuring kit
   d. In clean, closed containers
3. The most popular nail shape for men is
   a. Square
   b. Round
   c. Oval
   d. Pointed
4. When performing pedicures, you should work from
   a. Little toe to big toe
   b. Big toe to little toe
5. Before a paraffin wax treatment, a heat tolerance test should be performed by
   a. Sticking your hands into the paraffin wax
   b. Sticking your client's hands into the paraffin wax
   c. Pouring a little wax out to see if it will solidify within 30 seconds
   d. Drop a 1 inch size circle on the client's hands to see if it is well tolerated
6. What massage technique is most often used by nail technicians?
   a. Effleurage
   b. Petrissage
   c. Tapotement
   d. Vibration
7. In a massage technique called _____, skin tissue is lifted and pressed together.
   a. Effleurage
   b. Petrissage
   c. Tapotement
   d. Vibration
8. You should talk to your clients during massages to help them relax.
   a. True
   b. False
9. Some conditions require multiple appointments to resolve the issue. This is called a
   a. Set pedicure
   b. Multiple service pedicure
   c. Complex pedicure
   d. Series pedicure

10. Applying nail polish close to the eponychium will cause the polish to lift within a few days.
    a. True
    b. False
11. Before a pedicure appointment, women should avoid shaving their legs within _____ hours before the appointment.
    a. 12
    b. 24
    c. 48
    d. There is no need to avoid shaving
12. Sea sand, ground apricot kernels, and jojoba beads are examples of
    a. Acids
    b. Bases
    c. Exfoliating agents
    d. Moisturizers
13. Toe separators are single use items.
    a. True
    b. False
14. Which nail shape may break more easily and is more difficult to maintain?
    a. Square
    b. Squoval
    c. Round
    d. Oval
    e. Pointed
15. Benefits of a paraffin bath include ? Select all that apply.
    a. Increased moisturization
    b. Reduced pain and inflammation
    c. Increased circulation to joins
    d. Warmth and relaxation
16. When clipping long nails,
    a. Clip from one side to the other side
    b. Clip the sides and center in one clip
    c. Clip from the sides, clipping towards the center
17. Which of the following has the correct order of steps for performing a manicure?
    a. Remove polish from nails; apply cuticle remover, remove cuticles, and wash cuticle remover from hands; file and shape nails; soak the fingers; brush the nails with a nail brush; dry the hands; buff the nails; apply nail oil to nails; lotion and massage the hands; remove oil or lotion from the nail plate; apply polish
    b. Remove polish from nails; file and shape nails; soak the fingers; brush the nails with a nail brush; dry the hands; apply cuticle remover, remove cuticles, and wash cuticle remover from hands; buff the nails; apply nail oil to nails; lotion and massage the hands; remove oil or lotion from the nail plate; apply polish
    c. Remove polish from nails; file and shape nails; soak the fingers;  apply nail oil to nails; brush the nails with a nail brush; dry the hands; apply cuticle remover,

remove cuticles, and wash cuticle remover from hands; buff the nails; lotion and massage the hands; remove oil or lotion from the nail plate; apply polish

d. Remove polish from nails; file and shape nails; soak the fingers; dry the hands; brush the nails with a nail brush; apply cuticle remover, remove cuticles, and wash cuticle remover from hands; buff the nails; apply nail oil to nails; lotion and massage the hands; remove oil or lotion from the nail plate; apply polish

18. To remove nail oil from the nail plates, _____. Select all that apply.
    a. Use cotton saturated with alcohol
    b. Use cotton saturated with acetone or polish remover
    c. Use cotton saturated with water
    d. Use cotton saturated with cuticle remover

19. Before massaging the hands, you should apply enough lotion
    a. To moisturize the hands
    b. To make the hands very slippery
    c. To prevent skin drag

20. To help remove or lessen yellow stains or discoloration of the nails,
    a. Apply a clear coat to the nails
    b. Apply nail bleach
    c. Apply nail oil
    d. None of the above

21. When brushing nails with a nail brush, you should
    a. Use downward strokes, starting from the first knuckle and brushing towards the fingertips.
    b. Use upward strokes, starting from the fingertips and brushing towards the first knuckle
    c. Brush horizontally across the nail plate
    d. A and B

22. When using curettes, the bowl of the curette should face _____ the skin.
    a. Away from
    b. Toward

23. According to client surveys, the most enjoyable part of a pedicure is
    a. Having clean nails
    b. Having pretty nails
    c. The massage
    d. Having calluses removed

24. Before applying nail polish, you should ask clients to put on any jewelry or outerwear they took off before service.
    a. True
    b. False

25. Paraffin wax should be maintained at a temperature
    a. Below 100F
    b. Between 125 and 132F
    c. Between 132 and 140F
    d. Above 140F

26. When filing nails, you should
    a. Use a sawing back and forth motion
    b. File into the corners of the nails
    c. File from one side to the center and then file from the other side to the center
    d. B and C
27. In a massage technique called _____, the skin is rapidly tapped or striked by the hand.
    a. Effleurage
    b. Petrissage
    c. Tapotement
    d. Vibration
28. When performing a manicure, you should work from
    a. Pinky finger to thumb finger
    b. Thumb finger to pinky finger
29. During a paraffin wax treatment, the paraffin should remain on the hands for
    a. 5 to 10 minutes
    b. 15 to 20 minutes
    c. 25 to 30 minutes
    d. 60 minutes
30. What should be used to remove debris for toe nail folds, eponychium, and hyponychium areas?
    a. Toenail clippers
    b. Toenail nippers
    c. Curettes
    d. Nail rasp
31. Hot stones can transfer MRSA infections between clients.
    a. True
    b. False
32. Which tool can be used to reduce and smooth foot calluses?
    a. Curettes
    b. Nail rasp
    c. Toenail nippers
    d. Pedicure paddles
33. A complete manicured nail typically has how many coats?
    a. 1
    b. 2
    c. 3
    d. 4
34. Which tool can be used to reduce the sides of the free edge to reduce chances of an ingrown nail?
    a. Toenail clippers
    b. Nail rasp
    c. Foot files or pedicure paddles
    d. Nail files
35. Select all the true statements about a basic pedicure.

    a. Basic pedicures typically take 30 to 45 minutes

    b. Basic pedicures typically take 1 to 1.5 hours

    c. Basic pedicures include a foot massage

    d. Basic pedicures include a leg massage

36. Nail implements should be removed from their containers using _____ to prevent contamination.

    a. Two fingers

    b. Single use plastic or metal spatula

    c. Paper towels

    d. Cloth towel

37. The bottom of the foot is the only place a friction movement is used in a manicure and pedicure service.

    a. True

    b. False

38. The practice of _____ involves using essential oils to relax or invigorate the client.

    a. Reflexology

    b. Aromatherapy

    c. Dermatology

    d. Psychotherapy

39. The manicure service cushion should be _____throughout the service.

    a. Covered with a towel

    b. Covered with plastic

    c. Uncovered

40. Which nail file grit is best for toenails?

    a. Fine

    b. Small

    c. Medium

    d. Large

41. If a client decides to get a paraffin wax treatment before a manicure, soaking the hands in water is not necessary because the paraffin treatment already softens the skin.

    a. True

    b. False

42. Examples of conditions that require a series pedicure include? Select all that apply.

    a. Fungus nails

    b. Callus reduction

    c. Scaly feet

    d. Ingrown nails

43. In a massage technique called _____, the hands glide over a body part.

    a. Effleurage

    b. Petrissage

    c. Tapotement

    d. Vibration

44. Which nail shape is thought to be attractive on most women's hands?

    a. Square

b. Squoval

c. Round

d. Oval

e. Pointed

45. Products that are put into the water in a pedicure bath to soften the skin on the feet are called ?

a. Foot soaks

b. Foot scrubs

c. Foot lotions

d. Callus removers

46. Hot stones are typically made of

a. Salt

b. Basalt

c. Granite

d. Marble

47. Paraffin wax treatments should be avoided for? Select all that apply.

a. Clients with impaired circulation

b. Clients cuts or burns

c. Clients with rashes or eczema

d. Clients with warts

48. It is the responsibility of _____ to ensure proper infection control procedures are followed.

a. Nail technician

b. Salon

c. Client

d. Nail technician and salon

49. For ergonomic reasons, a nail technician's pedicuring stool should be

a. High

b. Low

50. For which one of the following are oil manicures recommended?

a. Leukonychia

b. Split nails

c. Brittle nails

d. Prevention of infection

51. Nails should be soaked in water before filing.

a. True

b. False

# Perform Application, Maintenance, and Removal Procedures for Nail Enhancement Services

1. Nail tips that are _____ require less filing on natural nails after application.
    a. Pre-beveled
    b. Pre-cut
    c. Well-less
    d. All of the above
2. UV gloss gels can be used over monomer and polymer enhancements.
    a. True
    b. False
3. To prevent damaging nail wraps when removing old polish, use
    a. A file to remove the old polish
    b. Use a non-acetone polish remover
    c. Use an acetone polish remover
    d. Use a resin softener first
4. Cutting tips with fingernail or toenail clippers can weaken tips and cause tips to crack.
    a. True
    b. False
5. High vibration during use of an electric file can ? Select all that apply.
    a. Cause microshattering of nail enhancement products
    b. Be harmful to the technicians hand, wrist, and arm
    c. Lead to the development of carpal tunnel syndrome
    d. None of the above
6. To repair tip separation, you must first remove the old nail enhancement product.
    a. True
    b. False
7. What are some "rings of fire" causes? Select all that apply.
    a. Keeping the bit parallel to the nail
    b. Using a flat tipped bit at an angle
    c. Using too low of a speed
    d. Not applying enough pressure
8. What are some ways to prevent grabbing during filing? Select all that apply.
    a. Keep the bit parallel to the nail
    b. Keep the bit angled to the nail
    c. Angle the bit to file the sides of the nail
    d. Angle the finger to file the sides of the nail
    e. Use bits with rounded ends
9. What are some causes of heat during filing? Select all that apply.
    a. Too much pressure
    b. Incorrect speed (RPM)
    c. Leaving the bit in one place for too long
    d. Using sanders or sleeves

    e. Lifting the bit too frequently

10. What resin should be used for clients who want colored polish or gel polish over an enhancement?
    a. Clear resin
    b. Pink resin
    c. White pigmented resin
    d. Tan resin

11. You should use nippers to trim or remove loose nail enhancement products.
    a. True
    b. False

12. During nail enhancement maintenance, what type of bit should be used to prepare for a backfill?
    a. Medium grit bit with a round-tipped edge
    b. Medium grit bit with a flat tipped edge
    c. Fine grit bit with a round-tipped edge
    d. Fine grit bit with a flat tipped edge

13. When applying UV gel, patting the brush or pressing too hard can? Select all that apply.
    a. Cause the UV gel to dry too quickly
    b. Introduce air into the gel
    c. Weaken the gel enhancement
    d. Make the gel enhancement too hard

14. High shine bits or buffer bits are single use only.
    a. True
    b. False

15. Nail tips have a shallow depression called a _____.
    a. Position stop
    b. Tip point
    c. Well
    d. Demarcation line

16. Which electric file bits should never be used on natural nails?
    a. Diamond bits
    b. Carbide bits
    c. Barrel bits
    d. UNC bits

17. The strongest nail wrap material is
    a. Silk
    b. Linen
    c. Fiberglass
    d. Paper

18. What should be used to correct flat fingernails?
    a. UV bonding gels
    b. UV building gels
    c. UV self leveling gels
    d. UV gel polish

19. To speed up the hardening process of a wrap resin or adhesive overlay, you should use
    a. A nail dehydrator
    b. UV lights
    c. A wrap resin accelerator or activator
    d. All of the above
20. In addition to the standard implements on a manicuring table, what supplies are needed for a nail tip application procedure? Select all that apply.
    a. Nail tips
    b. Nail tip adhesive
    c. Acetone
    d. Abrasive boards
    e. Tip cutter
    f. Wrap resin
    g. Buffer block
    h. Nail dehydrator
21. The first step in the nail tip removal procedure is to cut off the nail tip.
    a. True
    b. False
22. The advantages of nail wraps are they _____. Select all that apply.
    a. Decrease the time between maintenance periods
    b. Can increase the strength and durability of nail tips.
    c. Can be used to repair or strengthen natural nails
    d. Can be used to create nail extensions
23. Which UV gel is used to repair a crack in a nail enhancement?
    a. UV bonding gels
    b. UV building gels
    c. UV self leveling gels
    d. UV gel polishes
24. During nail wrap application, wrap resin should be applied _____.
    a. Over the entire surface of the nail and tip
    b. Over the entire surface of the nail
    c. Over the entire surface of the tip
    d. Where the nail tip meets the natural nail
25. What are the ways monomer liquid and polymer powder can be applied? Select all that apply.
    a. They can be applied as a protective overlay on the natural nail
    b. They can be applied over a nail tip
    c. They can be used to create a nail extension
    d. They can be used to hydrate the nail
26. Which bit works best for smoothing calluses?
    a. Small and large barrel bits
    b. Maintenance bits
    c. Needle bits
    d. Pedicure bits

27. Applying nail enhancement products over wet nail primers can cause the nail enhancement product to discolor and break down.
    a. True
    b. False
28. Which UV gel is used to increase adhesion to the natural nail?
    a. UV bonding gels
    b. UV building gels
    c. UV self leveling gels
    d. UV gel polishes
29. What consistency should the product bead have?
    a. Dry
    b. Wet
    c. Medium to dry
    d. Medium to wet
30. The amount of colored pigment in a gel is called
    a. Viscosity
    b. Pigmentation
    c. Clarity
    d. Opacity
31. UV gel polishes may be used on natural nails.
    a. True
    b. False
32. Monomer liquid and polymer power should be stored _____. Select all that apply.
    a. Away from each other
    b. In a covered container
    c. In a cool, dark area
    d. Near heat
33. What are some reasons why you should avoid using large brushes when working with monomer liquid and polymer powder? Select all that apply.
    a. Large brushes increase the risk that the brush touches the skin
    b. Large brushes can hold too much liquid
    c. Large brushes can increase the risk of improper liquid and powder ratio
    d. Only A and B
34. As nail enhancement products age, they can become brittle and develop tiny cracks. This is known as
    a. Brittle nails
    b. Cracked nails
    c. Macroshattering
    d. Microshattering
35. Monomer liquid should be poured into
    a. Open mouthed jars
    b. Containers with large openings
    c. A shallow bowl
    d. A dappen dish

36. What resin should be used for clients who want French or American manicure finish without using nail lacquer?
    a. Clear resin
    b. Pink resin
    c. White pigmented resin
    d. Pink resin and white pigmented resin
37. Nail wraps are a type of
    a. Nail tip
    b. Overlay
    c. Nail resin
    d. Nail adhesive
38. Nail tips are strong enough to wear on their own.
    a. True
    b. False
39. When applying UV or LED gel to the natural nail,
    a. Only the first layer of product needs to be cured
    b. Only the last layer of product needs to be cured
    c. Only the first and last layers of product needs to be cured
    d. Each layer of product needs to be cured
40. When not in use, UV brushes and gel containers should be ? Select all that apply.
    a. Stored away from windows
    b. Stored away from all sources of UV light
    c. Exposed to sunlight to prevent bacterial growth
    d. Stored away from full spectrum lights
41. Which UV gel is used to enhance the thickness of other gels and provide a smoother surface?
    a. UV bonding gels
    b. UV building gels
    c. UV self leveling gels
    d. UV gel polishes
42. After service, a dappen dish should be cleaned with
    a. Alcohol
    b. Acetone
    c. Hot water
    d. A lint free towel
43. Which bits can be used in the cuticle area? Select all that apply.
    a. Cuticle safety bits
    b. Cone shaped bits
    c. Football shaped bits
    d. Bullet bits
    e. Small and large barrel bits
44. The amount of UV light produced by UV lamps is called UV light
    a. Viscosity
    b. Opacity

c.  Intensity

d.  Power

45. Nail primer should be applied to plastic nail tips to improve adhesion to the natural nail.

    a.  True

    b.  False

46. What are the advantages of gel polish?

    a.  They are easier to remove than regular nail polish

    b.  They do not smudge

    c.  They do not thicken over time

    d.  B and C

47. What is the first step in performing a manicure?

    a.  Shape the nails

    b.  Soften the cuticles

    c.  Clean under free edge

    d.  Remove old polish

48. Hard and soft UV gels can both be removed using acetone

    a.  True

    b.  False

49. Less pressure should be used when filing UV and LED gel enhancements than monomer and polymer enhancements.

    a.  True

    b.  False

50. The advantages of pre beveled nail tips include

    a.  Requiring less filing of the natural nail

    b.  Lessens potential damage to the natural nail

    c.  A and b

    d.  None of the above

51. What should be used to remove oil from nails?

    a.  A lint free towel

    b.  A nail activator

    c.  Acetone

    d.  A nail dehydrator

52. Improper curing of UV or LED gel can lead to? Select all that apply.

    a.  Skin cancer

    b.  Service breakdown

    c.  Skin irritation

    d.  Skin sensitivity

53. The point where the nail tip is adhered to the natural nail is called the _____.

    a.  Position stop

    b.  Tip point

    c.  Well

    d.  Demarcation line

54. When removing the inhibition layer from the UV gel,

    a.  Wipe from the free edge of the fingernail towards the cuticle

    b. Wipe from the cuticle towards the free edge of the fingernail
55. What should be applied to a split in the nail before wrapping it?
    a. Top coat
    b. Base coat
    c. Adhesive glue
    d. Nail hardener
56. When blending the nail tip at the contact area, the file should be held
    a. At a 30 degree angle
    b. At a 45 degree angle
    c. At a 90 degree angle
    d. Flat to the nail
57. What is used as a guide to extend the nail enhancement beyond the fingertip?
    a. Nail form
    b. A ruler
    c. Metal pusher
    d. Wooden pusher
58. Free edge separation from nail enhancement products can be caused by ? Select all that apply.
    a. Nail enhancement product breakdown
    b. Aging of the nail enhancement product
    c. A client being hard on the nails
    d. Only A and B
59. During UV and LED gel maintenance, UV gel should be applied
    a. Only on the area of regrowth
    b. To the entire nail
60. When working with electric files with higher torque, you should work at _____ speeds.
    a. Higher
    b. Lower

# Perform Post-service Procedures

1. When making retail recommendations, what should you explain to the client? Select all that apply.
   a. What is being recommended
   b. Why you are recommending a product
   c. How the product should be used at home
   d. Who else uses the product

2. During post-service procedures, information should be recorded in a
   a. Client record form
   b. Client intake form
   c. Client questionnaire
   d. Client survey

3. Nail enhancements should be serviced
   a. After 1 or more weeks
   b. After 2 or more weeks
   c. After 3 or more weeks
   d. After 4 or more weeks

4. With proper home maintenance, how long should a nail polish application last?
   a. 3 to 5 days
   b. 7 to 10 days
   c. 14 to 21 days
   d. 21 to 31 days

5. You must wash your hands after removing gloves.
   a. True
   b. False

6. Clients should pay
   a. Before a procedure is performed
   b. After a procedure is performed

7. What type of information should be recorded after completing a procedure? Select all that apply.
   a. Products used
   b. Observations
   c. Products recommended
   d. Services performed

8. Which of the following is performed during post-service procedures? Select all that apply.
   a. Promoting products
   b. Scheduling the next appointment
   c. Thanking the client
   d. Disinfecting implements
   e. Reset the work area

9. The best time to recommend retail products to clients is
   a. During pre-service procedures

b. During the procedure
c. During post-service procedures

# Section 1 Answers

# Practice Exam 1 Answers

1. A. At least once a week.
2. E. Onychorrhexis is associated with brittle nails with lengthwise ridges. Beau's lines are depression lines that run the width of the nail plate; it often indicates a past major illness or injury. Plicatured nails are associated with highly curved nail plates. Eggshell nails are thin, weak, and flexible nail plates. Melanonychia is a darkening of the nail.
3. D. Melanocytes produce melanin which is responsible for skin coloring. Keratin is a protein found in hair and nails. Collagen gives the skin form and suppleness. Elastin gives skin its flexibility.
4. B. Lye is a very strong alkali that is often used as a callus softener.
5. A,B,C,D,E.
6. C. A suspension. Suspensions are a mixture of undissolved particles in liquid. Suspensions may separate over time and that is why particles in nail polish may separate over time. Emulsions are mixtures of two or more substances bounded by an emulsifier. Emulsions will eventually separate, but will do so very slowly and over a long period of time. Surfactants are often used as emulsifiers.
7. D. MRSA (Methicillin resistant staphylococcus aureus) is a common bacteria found in humans that can be highly resistant to certain antibiotics.
8. D. Organs are composed of specialized tissues that perform a specific function. The stomach is an organ.
9. B. Petrissage
10. D. Polymerization.
11. C,D.
12. C.
13. B. False. Nails should be filed before being soaked in water. Water will make the nails softer and easier to damage.
14. A. Nail form
15. D. Remove old polish
16. B. Acetone
17. A,B,C.
18. B. After 2 or more weeks
19. A. Pre-beveled
20. B. The palm of the hand is the metacarpus. The carpus is the wrist. Phalanges are the bones of the fingers or toes.
21. A. True
22. B. False. Each client must use a clean and disinfected nail brush to wash their hands.
23. B. Use a non-acetone polish remover
24. A. True. Always use tips clippers to clip tips.
25. A,B,C
26. A. True. To repair tip separation, you should first remove the old nail enhancement product, expose and prepare the natural nail, and reapply the primer and nail enhancement product.

27. B. Keeping the bit parallel to the nail and using low speeds and light pressure reduces the risk of "rings of fire".
28. A,D,E.
29. A,B,C,D. Lifting the bit frequently actually helps reduce heat.
30. A. Clear resin.
31. B. False. You should never use nippers to trim or remove loose nail enhancement products because it can cause the remaining enhancement product to pull away from the nail and damage the nail.
32. C. Catalysts.
33. A. Bed
34. A. Medium grit bit with a round-tipped edge. Use a medium grit bit to smooth the old product down to the natural nail.
35. B,C. UV gels do not dry, they cure. Patting the brush or pressing too hard does not make the gel enhancement too hard.
36. A. True
37. C. Well
38. B. Carbide bits have flutes that shave enhancement products and should never be used on natural nails.
39. B. Linen is considered the strongest wrap material; however, it is opaque and a colored polish must be used with it. A silk wrap is lightweight and transparent and is also very durable. Fiberglass wraps have great adhesion and clarity and are also very durable. Paper wraps are not as durable as fabric wraps.
40. B. UV building gels
41. C. A wrap resin accelerator or activator
42. A,B,D,E,G,H.  All items listed except acetone and wrap resin are needed for a nail tip application procedure. Acetone is used to remove nail tips, not apply them. Wrap resin is used for nail wrap application.
43. C. Cleansed and disinfected
44. B. Onychocryptosis. Onychia is an inflammation of the nail matrix. Onychomadesis is the separation of the nail plate from the nail matrix. Onychomycosis is a fungal infection.
45. D. In clean, closed containers
46. B. Matrix
47. B. A medium grit abrasive. Lower grit files are typically not used for natural nails. Higher grit files are used to remove scratches. Fine grit abrasives are used for polishing and removing very fine scratches.
48. A. Little toe to big toe.
49. D.
50. C,D. The peroneus brevis and soleus muscles help bend the foot down. The extensor digitorum longus and tibialis anterior muscles help bend the foot up.
51. B. False. The activated carbon filter must be at least 3 inches to effectively absorb vapors and remove them from the salon air.
52. A. Effleurage
53. A.True.

54. D. Series pedicure
55. A. True. Nail polish close to the eponychium or skin will lift within a few days due to the natural oils in skin.
56. C. 48 hours. Shaving the legs can create microscope cuts that allow microbes to penetrate the skin; women should avoid shaving for 48 hours before a pedicure appointment.
57. C. Exfoliating agents.
58. A. True. Since toe separators cannot be cleaned and disinfected, they must be discarded after use by a client.
59. E. Pointed
60. B. Striated muscles are under voluntary control. Non-striated, smooth, and cardiac muscles are under involuntary control.
61. A,B,C,D.
62. C. Clip from the sides, clipping towards the center; this prevents stressing the sides of the nail and reduces the risk of splitting the nail.
63. B. Remove polish from nails; file and shape nails; soak the fingers; brush the nails with a nail brush; dry the hands; apply cuticle remover, remove cuticles, and wash cuticle remover from hands; buff the nails; apply nail oil to nails; lotion and massage the hands; remove oil or lotion from the nail plate; apply polish
64. A. True
65. B. 20 seconds
66. A. An abrasive
67. C. Dimethylurea hardeners can be used to strengthen natural nails without overhardening nails. While methylene glycol hardeners also help strengthen nails, they should not be applied to brittle, rigid, or very hard nails because methylene glycol hardeners can over harden nails and cause nails to shatter. Protein hardeners do not strengthen nails; they only form a hard coating over nails.
68. C. Fingernails are replaced in 4 to 6 months. Toenails are replaced in 9 to 12 months.
69. C. Base coat.
70. E. Excessive use of cuticle removers can lead to dry skin, dry eponychium, and hangnails.
71. B. Nail oils and lotions are designed to be absorbed into nails and skin to make them more flexible and supple. Nail creams are designed to form a seal around the skin of nails to keep moisture in.
72. A,B,C,D.
73. A. True
74. A. True
75. A. True.
76. A,B,C,D,E. All of the above should be done during the client consultation. Review the client intake form to get a general overview of the client as well as review any contraindications. You should assess your client's hands and nails for any weaknesses as well as determine the ideal length and shape of nails. Ask about your client's career and hobbies to determine what nail styles would best suit them. The client consultation is also a good time to upsell services.

77. C. 20 seconds.
78. D.
79. A.True. Acids and alkalis neutralize each other when mixed together. Liquid soaps are acidic and callus softeners are alkaline.
80. B. False. While N95 masks are effective at filtering out dust particles, they are not effective against vapors.
81. B. A physical mixture. Colored powders are a mixture of pigments and powder.
82. A.Silicone
83. D. Monomer liquid and polymer powder systems use thermal initiators. UV curing products use photoinitiators.
84. A,B,C.
85. C. Solvent. A solution is a homogeneous mixture of two substances. A solute is the substance that is dissolved by the solvent to form a solution.
86. A.Physical
87. A.Extensors help the wrist, hand, and fingers to form a straight line. Flexors help bend the wrist. Pronators help turn the palm so that the palm faces downward. Supinators help turn the palm so the palm faces upward.
88. A,B,C,D.
89. A. Hangnails
90. A.True. Since contact dermatitis is caused by touching certain substances, avoiding contact with the substances will prevent contact dermatitis.
91. A,B,C,D.
92. B. False. The nail plate is porous and allows water to pass through to the nail bed.
93. D. The lunula.
94. C. Epithelial. Connective tissue is tissue that supports and connects other tissue and parts of the body. Epithelial tissues form the covering of all body parts and organs. Muscle tissue function by contracting. Nerve tissues carry signals between the brain and body parts.
95. B. False. Nail technicians are allowed to push back the eponychium, but are not allowed to cut the eponychium.
96. A,B,C.
97. A,B,D. Towels, bits, and some buffers are multi-use or reusable items. Pumice stones and wooden sticks are single-use or disposable items.
98. B. Disposal restrictions.
99. B. Treat minor cuts
100.   D. Logbook
101.   D. You are most likely to encounter Hepatitis B and C in a salon. Hepatitis A is more commonly associated with foodborne illnesses.
102.   A. Open
103.   C. Exposure incident.
104.   B. Round
105.   B. False. Hand sanitizers or antiseptics do not clean or remove debris; they are not a replacement for hand washing.

106. A. True.
107. B. False. Talking during a massage may hinder the client's relaxation.
108. A. True. Porous items that have been exposed to broken skin, blood, or body fluids must be thrown away. Do not try to disinfect them.
109. A. Client record form. The client intake form is filled out during pre-service procedures.
110. C. Diplococci is the bacteria most likely to cause pneumonia. Staphylococci can cause a wide range of infections including toxic shock syndrome. Streptococci is most commonly associated with strep throat and blood poisoning. Bacilli can cause diseases such as tetanus, tuberculosis, diphtheria, etc. Spirilla can be associated with syphilis, Lyme disease, etc.

# Practice Exam 2 Answers

1. B. Phenolics are a tuberculocidal disinfectant that can damage plastic and rubber and can cause some metals to rust. They should never be used to disinfect pedicure tubs or equipment.
2. C.
3. B. Glycerin
4. A,B,C,D.
5. D. Hives are examples of wheals. Wheals are itchy and swollen lesions. A cyst is a fluid filled sac. A vesicle is a blister. A macule is a spot of skin discoloration.
6. A.True. Although nail polish does not allow the growth of bacteria and any microbes in nail polish will die in a short period of time, microbes on nail polish brushes can be transferred if they are immediately used after the brush was contaminated.
7. A,B,C.
8. A. 5 to 10 minutes.
9. A,B,D. UV brushes and gel containers should be stored away from windows, full spectrum lights, and all sources of UV light or it will start to cure.
10. D. You are most likely to encounter Hepatitis B and C in a salon. Hepatitis A is more commonly associated with foodborne illnesses.
11. C. Fingernails are replaced in 4 to 6 months. Toenails are replaced in 9 to 12 months.
12. A,B,C,D.
13. A.Silicone
14. A,B,C,D.
15. A.True
16. B,C.
17. B. Petrissage
18. B. Carbide bits have flutes that shave enhancement products and should never be used on natural nails.
19. B. Keeping the bit parallel to the nail and using low speeds and light pressure reduces the risk of "rings of fire".
20. B. 7 to 10 days
21. A. True
22. B. After a procedure is performed.
23. B. 10 minutes.
24. C. The matrix is where nail plate cells are formed. The free edge is the part of the nail that protrudes over the nail bed. The nail bed is supplied with many blood vessels and nerves and supports the nail plate. Nail folds are skin that surround the nail plate.
25. B. False. Never cut off the nail because it can pull off layers of the natural nail. To remove nail tips, the first thing you should do is soak the client's fingers in acetone and then use a pusher to push off the softened nail tips.
26. B,C,D.
27. B. UV building gels
28. A. Over the entire surface of the nail and tip
29. A,B,C.

30. C. Subcutaneous
31. C. Tapotement
32. D. Pedicure bits
33. A. True
34. A. UV bonding gels
35. B. Hematoma. Keloid is a thick scar. An ulcer is an open sore on the skin with loss of skin depth. A fissure is a crack in the skin. An excoriation is a skin scratch or scrape. Scales are flakes of dry or oily skin.
36. C. Medium to dry
37. D. Opacity
38. A. True
39. A,B,C.
40. A,B,C.
41. D. Microshattering
42. B. A dappen dish. A dappen dish has a narrow opening to prevent evaporation of the monomer liquid. Open mouthed jars and containers with large openings will increase evaporation.
43. D. Pink resin and white pigmented resin
44. B. Overlay
45. B. False. The SDS Regulatory Information category lists agencies responsible for product regulation. The SDS Exposure Controls/Personal Protection category lists OSHA's permissible exposure limits and required personal protective equipment.
46. B. False. Nail tips are not strong enough to wear on their own and should be worn with an overlay.
47. C. The abductor hallucis is used to move the big toe. The flexor digiti minimi is used to move the little toe. The abductor digiti minimi is used to separate the toes.
48. D. Each layer of product needs to be cured.
49. A, B.
50. C. To prevent skin drag.
51. B. Apply nail bleach
52. A. Use downward strokes, starting from the first knuckle and brushing towards the fingertips.
53. B. Toward
54. B. The epidermis contains no blood vessels.
55. C. The massage.
56. A. True. By asking the clients to put on any jewelry or outerwear before applying nail polish, you can decrease the risk of smudges.
57. B. Between 125 and 132F
58. C. File from one side to the center and then file from the other side to the center. You should never use a sawing back and forth motion as this can cause the nail to split and peel. You should never file into the corners of the nails as this can increase the chance of developing ingrown nails.
59. A. Pinky finger to thumb finger
60. C. Curettes

61. C. The lymphatic or immune system is responsible for fighting disease and infection. The endocrine system produces and secretes hormones responsible for many functions, such as growth The integumentary system is composed of skin, hair, nails, and exocrine glands; it helps regulate body temperature and is the body's first line of defense. and sexual functions. The excretory system is responsible for the elimination of waste from the body; it includes organs such as the kidneys, liver, large intestine, and lungs.

62. A. True. Hot stones need to be cleaned and disinfected between clients to ensure they do not transfer pathogens from one client to another.

63. D. Pedicure paddles.

64. D. 4 coats: 1 base coat, 2 coats of nail polish, 1 top coat

65. B. Nail rasp

66. B. 40 to 60 watt. High temperatures from high-wattage incandescent bulbs can cause some nail enhancement products to cure too quickly, which can lead to cracking and lifting.

67. D. Put on gloves, wash implements with soap, rinse implements with warm water, soak implements in disinfectant, rinse and dry implements, store implements in a clean and dry container, remove gloves and wash your hands.

68. B. Stored in a clean and dry container until needed

69. A. True. Touch the doorknob with your hands can recontaminate the hands.

70. D. Fine grit abrasives have grits of 240 or higher. Lower grit abrasives have grits of 180 or lower. Medium grit abrasives have grits of 240. Higher grit abrasives have grits between 180 and 240.

71. B. Hepatitis B is the most difficult to kill, so you should check the disinfectant label to be sure it can be used to kill Hepatitis B.

72. B. File prepping.

73. C. Leukoderma is a skin disorder associated with light skin patches or absence of pigment. Lentigines are freckles. Chloasma are dark spots that are not elevated; also known as liver spots. Nevus is a mole.

74. D. Top coats prevent nail polish from chipping as well as provide a shine to the nails. Base coats prevent the nail plate from staining. Nail hardeners improve the strength of the nail plates. Nail oils improve the flexibility of the nail.

75. B.

76. B. False. Nail files and buffers are considered single-use items.

77. B. False. Shaking nail polish can cause air bubbles to form and cause an uneven texture. Instead of shaking, you should roll the nail polish bottle between your hands.

78. A,B,C,D,E.

79. A,B,C,D,E. Nails oils can support microbial growth; disposable brushes or droppers should be used to apply nail oil to nails.

80. B.

81. B.

82. A,B,C.

83. A. True

84. B. False. Acetone is highly flammable and should be kept away from heat and open flames.

85. D. All of the above.
86. B. False. Photoinitiators get energy when exposed to UV. Thermal initiators get energy from heat.
87. B. Cross-linked polymers. Products made from cross-linked polymers, such as nail enhancements, are much harder and do not dissolve easily. Non cross-linked polymers are easily dissolvable.
88. C. UV stabilizers.
89. B,C,D,E. When used properly, MMA is not toxic.
90. B. Immiscible. Immiscible liquids cannot be mixed into stable solutions; no matter how well you try to mix water and oil, they will always separate. Miscible liquids are liquids that can be mixed together and not easily separated.
91. A.True
92. A. Oligomers.
93. C. Matrix.
94. B. Eponychium. The dead tissue attached to the nail plate is called the cuticle.
95. B. False, The UV lamp wattage tells you the amount of electricity the lamp uses, not the amount of energy the lamp emits.
96. A,B,C,D. Repeated, prolonged, and long term exposure to substances (allergy-causing or not), can lead to contact dermatitis. Improper product consistency can also cause contact dermatitis. For example, beads that are too wet can work their way down to the nail bed and cause irritation. Undercuring UV or LED gel enhancements can also cause skin irritation.
97. B. Sebaceous glands secrete oil; blocked sebaceous glands can result in acne. Sudoriferous glands are sweat glands.
98. B,D,E. The foot is composed of tarsals, metatarsals, and phalanges.
99. B. False. Multi-use, or reusable items, can be cleaned and disinfected after exposure to blood or body fluids.
100.     D, E. You should always add a disinfectant to water (not water to disinfectant) to prevent foaming and thus an incorrect mixing ratio. The water used should be room temperature or cool, not hot.
101.     B. False. All tools must be completely immersed in disinfectant during the disinfection process.
102.     B. False. Leukonychia spots, or white spots, on the nail are due to damage or injury of the nail matrix; they do not indicate disease.
103.     A,B,C,D.
104.     B. False. Items should be cleaned to remove debris before they are disinfected. If debris is not removed first, the debris can interfere with the disinfectant.
105.     B. Feet.
106.     C. Standard precautions.
107.     C. UV self leveling gels
108.     B. At the end of every day.
109.     A.True. Since nail technicians are not allowed to perform medical procedures, nail technicians should never cut live skin or hardened tissue.
110.     D. Virus.

# Practice Exam 3 Answers

1. C. Medium grit nail files work best for toenails.
2. A,B,C,D,F.
3. A. True
4. C. Abductors are used to separate the fingers. Adductors are used to bring the fingers together. Pronators help turn the palm so that the palm faces downward. Supinators help turn the palm so the palm faces upward.
5. D. Plasticizers.
6. B. False.  The SDS Regulatory Information category lists agencies responsible for product regulation. The SDS Exposure Controls/Personal Protection category lists OSHA's permissible exposure limits and required personal protective equipment.
7. B,C. Nail enhancements and UV gel coatings. Coatings created by curing are examples of chemical reactions. Coatings created by evaporation are examples of physical reactions. Nail polish coatings are created through physical reactions.
8. A,B,C,D,E.
9. B. Eponychium. The dead tissue attached to the nail plate is called the cuticle.
10. B. False. Photoinitiators get energy when exposed to UV. Thermal initiators get energy from heat.
11. B. False. Shaking nail polish can cause air bubbles to form and cause an uneven texture. Instead of shaking, you should roll the nail polish bottle between your hands.
12. B. Nail rasp
13. A. True. Water can dilute the disinfectant solution.
14. B. Bone, cartilage, ligaments, and tendons are examples of connective tissue. Connective tissue is tissue that supports and connects other tissue and parts of the body.  Epithelial tissues form the covering of all body parts and organs. Muscle tissue function by contracting. Nerve tissues carry signals between the brain and body parts.
15. A.True. By asking the clients to put on any jewelry or outerwear before applying nail polish, you can decrease the risk of smudges.
16. B. Overlay
17. A. True
18. B. 7 to 10 days
19. A,B,C,D.
20. A,B,C,D,E.
21. C. UV self leveling gels
22. A,B,C,D,E.
23. B. Acetone
24. A,B,C,D. Small and large barrel bits should not be used in the cuticle area because they can cause "rings of fire" damage to the nails.
25. C. Intensity
26. B. False. Nail primer should only be applied to natural nails to improve adhesion.
27. D. Regular nail polish is easier to remove than gel polish
28. D. Remove old polish
29. A. True.

30. C.
31. D. Nail dehydrator
32. D. Organs are composed of specialized tissues that perform a specific function. The stomach is an organ.
33. A. Position stop
34. B. Wipe from the cuticle towards the free edge to prevent exposing the skin to the gel.
35. C. Adhesive glue
36. C. Disinfecting destroys or inactivates both the bacteria and viruses on hard, nonporous surfaces. Cleaning removes debris and dirt from a surface by scrubbing, washing, and rinsing. Sanitizing reduces the bacteria on surfaces. Sterilizing destroys all microorganisms, including spores.
37. D. Flat to the nail.
38. A. Nail form
39. A. Contagious. Contagious diseases can also be considered communicable.
40. A,B,C.
41. A,B,C,D,E,F,G.
42. B. To the entire nail
43. B. Lower. Machines with higher torque have more power so you should work at lower speeds.
44. A,C. Basic pedicures typically take 30 to 45 minutes and only include foot massages; they do not include leg massages. Spa pedicures typically take 1 to 1.5 hours and include foot and leg massages.
45. B. Single use plastic or metal spatula
46. A. True
47. B. Aromatherapy
48. A. Covered with a towel
49. A. True.
50. D. The femur is the thigh bone. The tibia is the shinbone; a larger bone that runs from the knee to the big-toe side of the ankle. The fibula is a smaller bone that runs from the knee to the pinky side of the ankle. The patella is the kneecap. The talus is the ankle bone.
51. B,C. Callus reductions and scaly feet may require a series pedicure to resolve the issue. Fungus nails and ingrown nails are not treated by nail technicians.
52. A. Effleurage
53. D. Oval
54. A. The lymphatic or immune system is responsible for fighting disease and infection. The endocrine system produces and secretes hormones responsible for many functions, such as growth and sexual functions. The integumentary system is composed of skin, hair, nails, and exocrine glands; it helps regulate body temperature and is the body's first line of defense. The excretory system is responsible for the elimination of waste from the body; it includes organs such as the kidneys, liver, large intestine, and lungs.
55. A. Foot soaks.
56. B. Basalt

57. A. True. Porous items that have been exposed to broken skin, blood, or body fluids must be thrown away. Do not try to disinfect them.
58. A,B,C,D
59. D. Nail technician and salon.
60. B. The pedicuring stool should be low to make it easier to work on a client's feet.
61. C. Brittle nails
62. B. False. Nails should be filed before being soaked in water. Water will make the nails softer and easier to damage.
63. D. 60 seconds
64. A. True
65. B. Ulna. The radius is a bone in the forearm that stretches from elbow to the thumb. The humerus is the arm bone that runs from the shoulder to the elbow. The eight bones of the carpus form the wrist.
66. B.
67. A.
68. A,B,C.
69. B,C,D.
70. E. Metal pushers, nail clippers, nail nippers, and tweezers are all multi-use implements.
71. C. Nail technicians should have at least 3 sets. One set in the disinfectant or autoclave, one set being used, and one set ready for use.
72. B. False. Lower grit abrasives can produce more visible scratches and should not be used on natural nails. Higher grit abrasives should be used on natural nails to smooth surfaces.
73. C,D.
74. A,B,D.
75. B. Physiology is the study of the functions of a body's structures. Anatomy is the study of the body's structures. Biology is the study of living organisms. Histology is the study of the microscopic structures of tissues.
76. C. The surface of a manicuring table should be made of a hard and impenetrable surface such as glass or Formica.
77. B,C. The nail technician's chair should have wheels that allow them to move around easily. The client's chair should NOT have wheels because chairs with wheels can be unstable and cause falls. The client's chair should have no or low side arms so that they can be moved closer to the table.
78. B. False. While hepatitis viruses can live on surfaces outside the body for long periods of time, the HIV virus does not.
79. A,B,C,E. Sexual orientation is not included in a client intake form.
80. A. True. You should get a written note from the client's physician to massage legs that suffer from varicose veins.
81. B. 5 to 15 minutes
82. C. Catalysts.
83. B. Acrylics.
84. A. True. Nail enhancement hardening occurs when monomers chain together to form polymers; this process can take up to 48 hours.

85. D. Polymerization.

86. B,C. Acetone and remover solvent will soften nail plates.

87. B. Chemical

88. B. Alkalis

89. A. Adhesives are chemicals that allow two surfaces to stick together. Nail primers improve adhesion between the nail and nail polish. Nail dehydrators are used to remove moisture and oil from the nails.

90. C. Repeated pressure on an area of the skin can cause it to develop into a callus. Calluses protect the skin from further damage.

91. B. Matrix

92. A.True. Fungal infections are contagious and you should not service clients with nail fungal infections.

93. B. Nail plate.

94. A.True

95. A,B,C,D. All of the above, except for "blood and nutrient circulation", are primary functions of the skeletal system. Blood and nutrient circulation are primary functions of the circulatory system.

96. A.Cells are the basic units of all living things. Cells are composed of a nucleus, protoplasm, cytoplasm, and cell membrane. Tissues are composed of cells that perform similar functions. Organs are composed of specialized tissues.

97. B. Indirect transmission is the transmission of body fluids through a contaminated object or surface. Direct transmission is the transmission of body fluids through touching, sneezing/coughing, or talking.

98. D. Chelating soaps.

99. B. False. You should never work on hands or feet that show signs of infection.

100.    D. MRSA (Methicillin resistant staphylococcus aureus) is a common bacteria found in humans that can be highly resistant to certain antibiotics.

101.    E. Expiration information is not found in the SDS The 16 categories of information found in the SDS are: Identification, Hazard Identification, Composition on Ingredients, First-aid Measures, Fire-fighting measures, Accidental Release Measures, Handling and Storage, Exposure controls/Personal Protection, Physical and Chemical Properties, Stability and Reactivity, Toxicology Information, Ecological Information, Disposal Consideration, Transport Information, Regulatory Information, and Revision Date.

102.    B. A joint is where two or more bones meet. A tendon connects muscle to bone.

103.    A. Salons may only use disinfectants approved and registered with the EPA.

104.    B. False. Some porous items such as towels and some nail files and buffers can be used on multiple clients.

105.    A.True

106.    B,C. Sanitizing and disinfecting are chemical processes. Cleaning is a physical process.

107.    B. The two steps are cleaning and disinfecting. The first step is cleaning. The second step is disinfecting.

108.    B. False. While soft UV gels may be removed using acetone, hard UV gels cannot.

109.    C. During post-service procedures

110.  C. Should be wiped dry with paper towels.

# Section 2 Answers

# Infection Control and Safety Practices Answers

1. A,B,D. Towels, bits, and some buffers are multi-use or reusable items. Pumice stones and wooden sticks are single-use or disposable items.
2. B. Disposal restrictions.
3. B. Treat minor cuts
4. C. 20 seconds.
5. A.True
6. D. Logbook
7. D. You are most likely to encounter Hepatitis B and C in a salon. Hepatitis A is more commonly associated with foodborne illnesses.
8. A. At least once a week.
9. A. Open
10. C. Exposure incident.
11. A,B,C,D,E.
12. B. False. Hand sanitizers or antiseptics do not clean or remove debris; they are not a replacement for hand washing.
13. A.True.
14. A.True. Porous items that have been exposed to broken skin, blood, or body fluids must be thrown away. Do not try to disinfect them.
15. C. Diplococci is the bacteria most likely to cause pneumonia. Staphylococci can cause a wide range of infections including toxic shock syndrome. Streptococci is most commonly associated with strep throat and blood poisoning. Bacilli can cause diseases such as tetanus, tuberculosis, diphtheria, etc. Spirilla can be associated with syphilis, Lyme disease, etc.
16. B. False. Multi-use, or reusable items, can be cleaned and disinfected after exposure to blood or body fluids.
17. D, E. You should always add a disinfectant to water (not water to disinfectant) to prevent foaming and thus an incorrect mixing ratio. The water used should be room temperature or cool, not hot.
18. B. Phenolics are a tuberculocidal disinfectant that can damage plastic and rubber and can cause some metals to rust. They should never be used to disinfect pedicure tubs or equipment.
19. B. 10 minutes.
20. B. False. All tools must be completely immersed in disinfectant during the disinfection process.
21. B. False. The SDS Regulatory Information category lists agencies responsible for product regulation. The SDS Exposure Controls/Personal Protection category lists OSHA's permissible exposure limits and required personal protective equipment.
22. A,B,C,D.
23. B. False. Items should be cleaned to remove debris before they are disinfected. If debris is not removed first, the debris can interfere with the disinfectant.
24. B. Feet.

25. C. Standard precautions.
26. B. Hepatitis B is the most difficult to kill, so you should check the disinfectant label to be sure it can be used to kill Hepatitis B.
27. B. At the end of every day.
28. A.True. Since nail technicians are not allowed to perform medical procedures, nail technicians should never cut live skin or hardened tissue.
29. B,C.
30. D. Virus.
31. B. Indirect transmission is the transmission of body fluids through a contaminated object or surface. Direct transmission is the transmission of body fluids through touching, sneezing/coughing, or talking.
32. A. True
33. D. Chelating soaps.
34. A.Contagious. Contagious diseases can also be considered communicable.
35. B. False. You should never work on hands or feet that show signs of infection.
36. A,B,C,D,F.
37. D. MRSA (Methicillin resistant staphylococcus aureus) is a common bacteria found in humans that can be highly resistant to certain antibiotics.
38. E. Expiration information is not found in the SDS. The 16 categories of information found in the SDS are: Identification, Hazard Identification, Composition on Ingredients, First-aid Measures, Fire-fighting measures, Accidental Release Measures, Handling and Storage, Exposure controls/Personal Protection, Physical and Chemical Properties, Stability and Reactivity, Toxicology Information, Ecological Information, Disposal Consideration, Transport Information, Regulatory Information, and Revision Date.
39. A. Salons may only use disinfectants approved and registered with the EPA.
40. A. True.
41. B. False. Some porous items such as towels and some nail files and buffers can be used on multiple clients.
42. B,C. Sanitizing and disinfecting are chemical processes. Cleaning is a physical process.
43. C. Disinfecting destroys or inactivates both the bacteria and viruses on hard, nonporous surfaces. Cleaning removes debris and dirt from a surface by scrubbing, washing, and rinsing.Sanitizing reduces the bacteria on surfaces. Sterilizing destroys all microorganisms, including spores.
44. B. False. While hepatitis viruses can live on surfaces outside the body for long periods of time, the HIV virus does not.
45. B. The two steps are cleaning and disinfecting. The first step is cleaning. The second step is disinfecting.
46. C. Should be wiped dry with paper towels.

# Human Anatomy and Physiology Answers

1. A. Extensors help the wrist, hand, and fingers to form a straight line. Flexors help bend the wrist. Pronators help turn the palm so that the palm faces downward. Supinators help turn the palm so the palm faces upward.

2. D. Melanocytes produce melanin which is responsible for skin coloring. Keratin is a protein found in hair and nails. Collagen gives the skin form and suppleness. Elastin gives skin its flexibility.

3. A,B,C,D.

4. A. Bed

5. B. The palm of the hand is the metacarpus. The carpus is the wrist. Phalanges are the bones of the fingers or toes.

6. A. Hangnails

7. C,D. The peroneus brevis and soleus muscles help bend the foot down. The extensor digitorum longus and tibialis anterior muscles help bend the foot up.

8. B. Onychocryptosis. Onychia is an inflammation of the nail matrix. Onychomadesis is the separation of the nail plate from the nail matrix. Onychomycosis is a fungal infection.

9. A. True. Since contact dermatitis is caused by touching certain substances, avoiding contact with the substances will prevent contact dermatitis.

10. A,B,C,D.

11. B. False. The nail plate is porous and allows water to pass through to the nail bed.

12. B. Striated muscles are under voluntary control. Non-striated, smooth, and cardiac muscles are under involuntary control.

13. C. Fingernails are replaced in 4 to 6 months. Toenails are replaced in 9 to 12 months.

14. D. The lunula.

15. E. Onychorrhexis is associated with brittle nails with lengthwise ridges. Beau's lines are depression lines that run the width of the nail plate; it often indicates a past major illness or injury. Plicatured nails are associated with highly curved nail plates. Eggshell nails are thin, weak, and flexible nail plates. Melanonychia is a darkening of the nail.

16. C. Epithelial. Connective tissue is tissue that supports and connects other tissue and parts of the body. Epithelial tissues form the covering of all body parts and organs. Muscle tissue function by contracting. Nerve tissues carry signals between the brain and body parts.

17. B. False. Nail technicians are allowed to push back the eponychium, but are not allowed to cut the eponychium.

18. C. Matrix.

19. C.

20. B. Eponychium. The dead tissue attached to the nail plate is called the cuticle.

21. C. The matrix is where nail plate cells are formed. The free edge is the part of the nail that protrudes over the nail bed. The nail bed is supplied with many blood vessels and nerves and supports the nail plate. Nail folds are skin that surround the nail plate.

22. C. The lymphatic or immune system is responsible for fighting disease and infection. The endocrine system produces and secretes hormones responsible for many functions, such as growthThe integumentary system is composed of skin, hair, nails, and exocrine

glands; it helps regulate body temperature and is the body's first line of defense. and sexual functions. The excretory system is responsible for the elimination of waste from the body; it includes organs such as the kidneys, liver, large intestine, and lungs.

23. C. The abductor hallucis is used to move the big toe. The flexor digiti minimi is used to move the little toe. The abductor digiti minimi is used to separate the toes.

24. B. False, The UV lamp wattage tells you the amount of electricity the lamp uses, not the amount of energy the lamp emits.

25. A,B,C,D. Repeated, prolonged, and long term exposure to substances (allergy-causing or not), can lead to contact dermatitis. Improper product consistency can also cause contact dermatitis. For example, beads that are too wet can work their way down to the nail bed and cause irritation. Undercuring UV or LED gel enhancements can also cause skin irritation.

26. C. Leukoderma is a skin disorder associated with light skin patches or absence of pigment. Lentigines are freckles. Chloasma are dark spots that are not elevated; also known as liver spots. Nevus is a mole.

27. B. False. Leukonychia spots, or white spots, on the nail are due to damage or injury of the nail matrix; they do not indicate disease.

28. B. Hematoma. Keloid is a thick scar. An ulcer is an open sore on the skin with loss of skin depth. A fissure is a crack in the skin. An excoriation is a skin scratch or scrape. Scales are flakes of dry or oily skin.

29. D. Hives are examples of wheals. Wheals are itchy and swollen lesions. A cyst is a fluid filled sac. A vesicle is a blister. A macule is a spot of skin discoloration.

30. A,B,C,D,E.

31. B. Sebaceous glands secrete oil; blocked sebaceous glands can result in acne. Sudoriferous glands are sweat glands.

32. B,D,E. The foot is composed of tarsals, metatarsals, and phalanges.

33. C. Subcutaneous

34. B. The epidermis contains no blood vessels.

35. C. Repeated pressure on an area of the skin can cause it to develop into a callus. Calluses protect the skin from further damage.

36. A,B,C,D,E,F,G.

37. C. Abductors are used to separate the fingers. Adductors are used to bring the fingers together. Pronators help turn the palm so that the palm faces downward. Supinators help turn the palm so the palm faces upward.

38. B. Matrix

39. A,B,C,D,E.

40. A.True. Fungal infections are contagious and you should not service clients with nail fungal infections.

41. B. Nail plate.

42. D. The femur is the thigh bone. The tibia is the shinbone; a larger bone that runs from the knee to the big-toe side of the ankle. The fibula is a smaller bone that runs from the knee to the pinky side of the ankle. The patella is the kneecap. The talus is the ankle bone.

43. A. True
44. B. Ulna. The radius is a bone in the forearm that stretches from elbow to the thumb. The humerus is the arm bone that runs from the shoulder to the elbow. The eight bones of the carpus form the wrist.
45. B. A joint is where two or more bones meet. A tendon connects muscle to bone.
46. A,B,C,D. All of the above, except for "blood and nutrient circulation", are primary functions of the skeletal system. Blood and nutrient circulation are primary functions of the circulatory system.
47. A. The lymphatic or immune system is responsible for fighting disease and infection. The endocrine system produces and secretes hormones responsible for many functions, such as growth and sexual functions. The integumentary system is composed of skin, hair, nails, and exocrine glands; it helps regulate body temperature and is the body's first line of defense. The excretory system is responsible for the elimination of waste from the body; it includes organs such as the kidneys, liver, large intestine, and lungs.
48. D. Organs are composed of specialized tissues that perform a specific function. The stomach is an organ.
49. B. Bone, cartilage, ligaments, and tendons are examples of connective tissue. Connective tissue is tissue that supports and connects other tissue and parts of the body. Epithelial tissues form the covering of all body parts and organs. Muscle tissue function by contracting. Nerve tissues carry signals between the brain and body parts.
50. A. Cells are the basic units of all living things. Cells are composed of a nucleus, protoplasm, cytoplasm, and cell membrane. Tissues are composed of cells that perform similar functions. Organs are composed of specialized tissues.
51. B. Physiology is the study of the functions of a body's structures. Anatomy is the study of the body's structures. Biology is the study of living organisms. Histology is the study of the microscopic structures of tissues.

# Chemistry of Nail Products Answers

1. A.True. Acids and alkalis neutralize each other when mixed together. Liquid soaps are acidic and callus softeners are alkaline.
2. B. False.  While N95 masks are effective at filtering out dust particles, they are not effective against vapors.
3. B. A physical mixture. Colored powders are a mixture of pigments and powder.
4. A.Silicone
5. D. Monomer liquid and polymer powder systems use thermal initiators. UV curing products use photoinitiators.
6. A,B,C.
7. C. Solvent. A solution is a homogeneous mixture of two substances. A solute is the substance that is dissolved by the solvent to form a solution.
8. C. A suspension. Suspensions are a mixture of undissolved particles in liquid. Suspensions may separate over time and that is why particles in nail polish may separate over time. Emulsions are mixtures of two or more substances bounded by an emulsifier. Emulsions will eventually separate, but wil do so very slowly and over a long period of time. Surfactants are often used as emulsifiers.
9. A.Physical
10. B. False. The activated carbon filter must be at least 3 inches to effectively absorb vapors and remove them from the salon air.
11. B. Lye is a very strong alkali that is often used as a callus softener.
12. A.True
13. B. False.  Acetone is highly flammable and should be kept away from heat and open flames.
14. D. All of the above.
15. B. False. Photoinitiators get energy when exposed to UV. Thermal initiators get energy from heat.
16. B. Cross-linked polymers. Products made from cross-linked polymers, such as nail enhancements, are much harder and do not dissolve easily.  Non cross-linked polymers are easily dissolvable.
17. C. UV stabilizers.
18. B,C,D,E. When used properly, MMA is not toxic.
19. B. Immiscible. Immiscible liquids cannot be mixed into stable solutions; no matter how well you try to mix water and oil, they will always separate. Miscible liquids are liquids that can be mixed together and not easily separated.
20. B. Glycerin
21. A.True
22. A. Oligomers.
23. C. Catalysts.
24. B. Acrylics.
25. A.True. Nail enhancement hardening occurs when monomers chain together to form polymers; this process can take up to 48 hours.
26. D. Polymerization.

27. B,C. Acetone and remover solvent will soften nail plates.
28. B. Chemical
29. B,C. Nail enhancements and UV gel coatings. Coatings created by curing are examples of chemical reactions. Coatings created by evaporation are examples of physical reactions. Nail polish coatings are created through physical reactions.
30. B. Alkalis
31. D. Plasticizers.
32. A. Adhesives are chemicals that allow two surfaces to stick together. Nail primers improve adhesion between the nail and nail polish. Nail dehydrators are used to remove moisture and oil from the nails.

# Client Consultation and Documentation Answers

1. C.
2. A,B,C,D,E.  All of the above should be done during the client consultation. Review the client intake form to get a general overview of the client as well as review any contraindications. You should assess your client's hands and nails for any weaknesses as well as determine the ideal length and shape of nails. Ask about your client's career and hobbies to determine what nail styles would best suit them. The client consultation is also a good time to upsell services.
3. D.
4. A,B,C.
5. B.
6. A,B,C.
7. A,B,C,D.
8. A,B,C,E.  Sexual orientation is not included in a client intake form.
9. A. True. You should get a written note from the client's physician to massage legs that suffer from varicose veins.
10. B. 5 to 15 minutes

# Nail Service Tools Answers

1. A. An abrasive
2. B. A medium grit abrasive. Lower grit files are typically not used for natural nails. Higher grit files are used to remove scratches. Fine grit abrasives are used for polishing and removing very fine scratches.
3. C. Dimethylurea hardeners can be used to strengthen natural nails without overhardening nails. While methylene glycol hardeners also help strengthen nails, they should not be applied to brittle, rigid, or very hard nails because methylene glycol hardeners can over harden nails and cause nails to shatter. Protein hardeners do not strengthen nails; they only form a hard coating over nails.
4. C. Base coat.
5. E. Excessive use of cuticle removers can lead to dry skin, dry eponychium, and hangnails.
6. B. Nail oils and lotions are designed to be absorbed into nails and skin to make them more flexible and supple. Nail creams are designed to form a seal around the skin of nails to keep moisture in.
7. A,B,C,D.
8. A. True
9. A. True.
10. D. Fine grit abrasives have grits of 240 or higher. Lower grit abrasives have grits of 180 or lower. Medium grit abrasives have grits of 240. Higher grit abrasives have grits between 180 and 240.
11. B. File prepping.
12. D. Top coats prevent nail polish from chipping as well as provide a shine to the nails. Base coats prevent the nail plate from staining. Nail hardeners improve the strength of the nail plates. Nail oils improve the flexibility of the nail.
13. B.
14. B. False. Nail files and buffers are considered single-use items.
15. B. False. Shaking nail polish can cause air bubbles to form and cause an uneven texture. Instead of shaking, you should roll the nail polish bottle between your hands.
16. A,B,C,D,E. Nails oils can support microbial growth; disposable brushes or droppers should be used to apply nail oil to nails.
17. A.True. Although nail polish does not allow the growth of bacteria and any microbes in nail polish will die in a short period of time, microbes on nail polish brushes can be transferred if they are immediately used after the brush was contaminated.
18. B.
19. A.
20. A,B,C.
21. E. Metal pushers, nail clippers, nail nippers, and tweezers are all multi-use implements.
22. C. Nail technicians should have at least 3 sets. One set in the disinfectant or autoclave, one set being used, and one set ready for use.

23. B. False. Lower grit abrasives can produce more visible scratches and should not be used on natural nails. Higher grit abrasives should be used on natural nails to smooth surfaces.
24. C,D.
25. A,B,D.
26. C. The surface of a manicuring table should be made of a hard and impenetrable surface such as glass or Formica.
27. B,C. The nail technician's chair should have wheels that allow them to move around easily. The client's chair should NOT have wheels because chairs with wheels can be unstable and cause falls. The client's chair should have no or low side arms so that they can be moved closer to the table.

# Nail Service Preparation Answers

1. A. True
2. B. False. Each client must use a clean and disinfected nail brush to wash their hands.
3. B. 20 seconds
4. B. 40 to 60 watt. High temperatures from high-wattage incandescent bulbs can cause some nail enhancement products to cure too quickly, which can lead to cracking and lifting.
5. D. Put on gloves, wash implements with soap, rinse implements with warm water, soak implements in disinfectant, rinse and dry implements, store implements in a clean and dry container, remove gloves and wash your hands.
6. B. Stored in a clean and dry container until needed
7. A. True. Touch the doorknob with your hands can recontaminate the hands.
8. D. 60 seconds
9. A. True
10. A. True

# Manicure and Pedicure Services Answers

1. C. Cleansed and disinfected
2. D. In clean, closed containers
3. B. Round
4. A. Little toe to big toe.
5. D.
6. A. Effleurage
7. B. Petrissage
8. B. False. Talking during a massage may hinder the client's relaxation.
9. D. Series pedicure
10. A.True. Nail polish close to the eponychium or skin will lift within a few days due to the natural oils in skin.
11. C. 48 hours. Shaving the legs can create microscope cuts that allow microbes to penetrate the skin; women should avoid shaving for 48 hours before a pedicure appointment.
12. C. Exfoliating agents.
13. A.True. Since toe separators cannot be cleaned and disinfected, they must be discarded after use by a client.
14. E. Pointed
15. A,B,C,D.
16. C. Clip from the sides, clipping towards the center; this prevents stressing the sides of the nail and reduces the risk of splitting the nail.
17. B. Remove polish from nails; file and shape nails; soak the fingers; brush the nails with a nail brush; dry the hands; apply cuticle remover, remove cuticles, and wash cuticle remover from hands; buff the nails; apply nail oil to nails; lotion and massage the hands; remove oil or lotion from the nail plate; apply polish
18. A, B.
19. C. To prevent skin drag.
20. B. Apply nail bleach
21. A.Use downward strokes, starting from the first knuckle and brushing towards the fingertips.
22. B. Toward
23. C. The massage.
24. A.True. By asking the clients to put on any jewelry or outerwear before applying nail polish, you can decrease the risk of smudges.
25. B. Between 125 and 132F
26. C.File from one side to the center and then file from the other side to the center. You should never use a sawing back and forth motion as this can cause the nail to split and peel. You should never file into the corners of the nails as this can increase the chance of developing ingrown nails.
27. C. Tapotement
28. A. Pinky finger to thumb finger
29. A. 5 to 10 minutes.

30. C. Curettes
31. A.True. Hot stones need to be cleaned and disinfected between clients to ensure they do not transfer pathogens from one client to another.
32. D. Pedicure paddles.
33. D. 4 coats: 1 base coat, 2 coats of nail polish, 1 top coat
34. B. Nail rasp
35. A,C. Basic pedicures typically take 30 to 45 minutes and only include foot massages; they do not include leg massages. Spa pedicures typically take 1 to 1.5 hours and include foot and leg massages.
36. B. Single use plastic or metal spatula
37. A. True
38. B. Aromatherapy
39. A. Covered with a towel
40. C. Medium grit nail files work best for toenails.
41. A.True.
42. B,C. Callus reductions and scaly feet may require a series pedicure to resolve the issue. Fungus nails and ingrown nails are not treated by nail technicians.
43. A. Effleurage
44. D. Oval
45. A. Foot soaks.
46. B. Basalt
47. A,B,C,D
48. D. Nail technician and salon.
49. B. The pedicuring stool should be low to make it easier to work on a client's feet.
50. C. Brittle nails
51. B. False. Nails should be filed before being soaked in water. Water will make the nails softer and easier to damage.

# Perform Application, Maintenance, and Removal Procedures for Nail Enhancement Services Answers

1. A. Pre-beveled
2. A. True
3. B. Use a non-acetone polish remover
4. A. True. Always use tips clippers to clip tips.
5. A,B,C
6. A. True. To repair tip separation, you should first remove the old nail enhancement product, expose and prepare the natural nail, and reapply the primer and nail enhancement product.
7. B. Keeping the bit parallel to the nail and using low speeds and light pressure reduces the risk of "rings of fire".
8. A,D,E.
9. A,B,C,D. Lifting the bit frequently actually helps reduce heat.
10. A. Clear resin.
11. B. False. You should never use nippers to trim or remove loose nail enhancement products because it can cause the remaining enhancement product to pull away from the nail and damage the nail.
12. A. Medium grit bit with a round-tipped edge. Use a medium grit bit to smooth the old product down to the natural nail.
13. B,C. UV gels do not dry, they cure. Patting the brush or pressing too hard does not make the gel enhancement too hard.
14. A. True
15. C. Well
16. B. Carbide bits have flutes that shave enhancement products and should never be used on natural nails.
17. B. Linen is considered the strongest wrap material; however, it is opaque and a colored polish must be used with it. A silk wrap is lightweight and transparent and is also very durable. Fiberglass wraps have great adhesion and clarity and are also very durable. Paper wraps are not as durable as fabric wraps.
18. B. UV building gels
19. C. A wrap resin accelerator or activator
20. A,B,D,E,G,H. All items listed except acetone and wrap resin are needed for a nail tip application procedure. Acetone is used to remove nail tips, not apply them. Wrap resin is used for nail wrap application.
21. B. False. Never cut off the nail because it can pull off layers of the natural nail. To remove nail tips, the first thing you should do is soak the client's fingers in acetone and then use a pusher to push off the softened nail tips.
22. B,C,D.
23. B. UV building gels
24. A. Over the entire surface of the nail and tip
25. A,B,C.

26. D. Pedicure bits
27. A. True
28. A. UV bonding gels
29. C. Medium to dry
30. D. Opacity
31. A. True
32. A,B,C.
33. A,B,C.
34. D. Microshattering
35. B. A dappen dish. A dappen dish has a narrow opening to prevent evaporation of the monomer liquid. Open mouthed jars and containers with large openings will increase evaporation.
36. D. Pink resin and white pigmented resin
37. B. Overlay
38. B. False. Nail tips are not strong enough to wear on their own and should be worn with an overlay.
39. D. Each layer of product needs to be cured.
40. A,B,D. UV brushes and gel containers should be stored away from windows, full spectrum lights, and all sources of UV light or it will start to cure.
41. C. UV self leveling gels
42. B. Acetone
43. A,B,C,D. Small and large barrel bits should not be used in the cuticle area because they can cause "rings of fire" damage to the nails.
44. C. Intensity
45. B. False. Nail primer should only be applied to natural nails to improve adhesion.
46. D. Regular nail polish is easier to remove than gel polish
47. D. Remove old polish
48. B. False. While soft UV gels may be removed using acetone, hard UV gels cannot.
49. A. True.
50. C.
51. D. Nail dehydrator
52. B,C,D.
53. A. Position stop
54. B. Wipe from the cuticle towards the free edge to prevent exposing the skin to the gel.
55. C. Adhesive glue
56. D. Flat to the nail.
57. A. Nail form
58. A,B,C.
59. B. To the entire nail
60. B. Lower. Machines with higher torque have more power so you should work at lower speeds.

# Perform Post-service Procedures Answers

1. A,B,C.
2. A. Client record form.  The client intake form is filled out during pre-service procedures.
3. B. After 2 or more weeks
4. B. 7 to 10 days
5. A. True
6. B. After a procedure is performed.
7. A,B,C,D.
8. A,B,C,D,E.
9. C. During post-service procedures

Printed in Great Britain
by Amazon

54096875R00066